FEMININE
SEXUALITY

By Jacques Lacan
in Norton Paperback

ÉCRITS: A SELECTION

FEMININE SEXUALITY

THE FOUR FUNDAMENTAL CONCEPTS
OF PSYCHO-ANALYSIS

THE SEMINAR OF JACQUES LACAN, BOOK I
Freud's Papers on Technique, 1953–1954

THE SEMINAR OF JACQUES LACAN, BOOK II
The Ego in Freud's Theory and in the Technique of
Psychoanalysis, 1954–1955

FEMININE SEXUALITY

Jacques Lacan
and the *école freudienne*

Edited by Juliet Mitchell and Jacqueline Rose

Translated by Jacqueline Rose

W · W · NORTON & COMPANY · *NEW YORK* · *LONDON*

PANTHEON BOOKS · *NEW YORK*

Printed in the United States of America.

First published in paperback 1985 by W. W. Norton and Pantheon Books.

Library of Congress Cataloging in Publication Data
Lacan, Jacques, 1901–
  Feminine sexuality.
  Bibliography: p.
  Includes index.
  I. Sex (Psychology)—Addresses, essays, lec-
tures.   2. Women—Psychology—Addresses, essays,
lectures.   3. Psychoanalysis—France—Addresses,
essays, lectures.   4. Lacan, Jacques, 1901–
I. Mitchell, Juliet, 1940–   II. Rose,
Jacqueline.   III. Title.
HQ21.L15213   1983   155.3'33   82–14546

ISBN 0-393-30211-3

W.W. Norton & Company, Inc.
500 Fifth Avenue, New York, N.Y. 10110
W.W. Norton & Company, Ltd
10 Coptic Street, London WC1A 1PU

Contents

Editors' Preface

The articles translated here are a selection put together by us in 1975 from the works of the French psychoanalyst, Jacques Lacan, and the *école freudienne*, the school of psychoanalysis which he directed in Paris between 1964 and 1980. They have never appeared together before, and only one has been translated previously into English. In making this selection our objective has been to show the relevance of Lacan's ideas for the continuing debate on femininity within both psychoanalysis and feminism.

Lacan's relationship to the psychoanalytic institution has always been controversial; his work became controversial for feminism when, in the 1970s, he focused more intensively on the question of feminine sexuality. In the years prior to his death in September 1981 both these controversies intensified.

The basic premise of Lacan's work is a questioning of any certainty or authority in notions of psychic and sexual life. There is a connection between this premise and his repeated breaks with psychoanalytic institutions. In January 1980 Lacan unilaterally dissolved the *école freudienne* in order to stop what he saw as the degradation of his ideas under the weight of his own institution. But this act, like Lacan's presentation of his work, was a challenge to authority yet at the same time authoritarian and patriarchal. It will be clear to the reader in the texts which follow that Lacan was trapped in the circles of this paradox.

The texts are preceded by an Introduction. In the first part, Juliet Mitchell situates Lacan's work in relation to his overall project within psychoanalytic theory, and then gives an account of the earlier psychoanalytic debate on femininity in the 1920s and 1930s of which these texts are in many ways the direct sequel. In the second part, Jacqueline Rose describes the conceptual movement of the texts themselves, and the implications of the debate on femininity in and around the work of Lacan. Although each part can be read separately, the Introduction as a whole represents a double engagement expressing our shared sense of the importance of Lacan for psychoanalysis, and of psycho-analysis for feminism.

Acknowledgements

We would like to thank Sally Alexander and George Craig.

J. M.
J. R.

January 1982

List of Abbreviations

PF *The Pelican Freud Library* (Harmondsworth: Penguin).
IJPA *International Journal of Psychoanalysis* (bulletin
of the International Psychoanalytical Association,
London).
PQ *Psychoanalytic Quarterly*.
IT 'Intervention on Transference'.
MP 'The Meaning of the Phallus'.
C 'Guiding Remarks for a Congress on Feminine
Sexuality'.
PP 'The Phallic Phase and the Subjective Import of the
Castration Complex'.
FS 'Feminine Sexuality in Psychoanalytic Doctrine'.
E 'God and the *Jouissance* of ~~The~~ Woman'⎱
  'A Love Letter'   ⎰ *Encore*.
O 'Seminar of 21 January 1975'.

References to Freud, by volume number, year of first publication
of article and page number, unless otherwise stated are to *The
Standard Edition of the Complete Psychological Works of Sigmund
Freud*, 24 vols (London: Hogarth, 1953–74). References to works
other than Lacan's seminars and *Ecrits* are given by author and
date. References to Lacan's seminars are by their seminar number
(for example, SXX), and to *Ecrits* as *Ecrits* with the earliest date of
publication or presentation of the article in parenthesis; the page
number to translations of articles which have already appeared in
English is provided in italics after the original page number,
although the translations might have been slightly modified. Full
bibliographical information is given at the beginning of each
translated text and in the general bibliography at the end of the
collection.

FEMININE
SEXUALITY

INTRODUCTION – I
Juliet Mitchell

> I object to all of you (Horney, Jones, Rado, etc.,) to the extent that you do not distinguish more clearly and cleanly between what is psychic and what is biological, that you try to establish a neat parallelism between the two and that you, motivated by such intent, unthinkingly construe psychic facts which are unprovable and that you, in the process of doing so, must declare as reactive or regressive much that without doubt is primary. Of course, these reproaches must remain obscure. In addition, I would only like to emphasize that we must keep psychoanalysis separate from biology just as we have kept it separate from anatomy and physiology . . . .
>
> (Freud, letter to Carl Müller-Braunschweig, 1935)

Jacques Lacan dedicated himself to the task of refinding and reformulating the work of Sigmund Freud. Psychoanalytic theory today is a variegated discipline. There are contradictions within Freud's writings and subsequent analysts have developed one aspect and rejected another, thereby using one theme as a jumping off point for a new theory. Lacan conceived his own project differently: despite the contradictions and impasses, there is a coherent theorist in Freud whose ideas do not need to be diverged from; rather they should be set within a cohesive framework that they anticipated but which, for historical reasons, Freud himself could not formulate. The development of linguistic science provides this framework.

It is certainly arguable that from the way psychoanalysis has grown during this century we have gained a wider range of therapeutic understanding and the multiplication of fruitful ideas, but we have lost the possibility of a clarification of an essential theory. To say that Freud's work contains contradictions should not be the equivalent of arguing that it is heterogeneous and that it is therefore legitimate for everyone to take their pick and develop it as they wish. Lacan set his face against

what he saw as such illegitimate and over-tolerant notions of
more-or-less peacefully co-existent lines of psychoanalytic
thought. From the outset he went back to Freud's basic concepts.
Here, initially, there is agreement among psychoanalysts as to
the terrain on which they work: psychoanalysis is about human
sexuality and the unconscious.

The psychoanalytic concept of sexuality confronts head-on all
popular conceptions. It can never be equated with genitality nor
is it the simple expression of a biological drive. It is always psychosexuality, a system of conscious and unconscious human fantasies involving a range of excitations and activities that produce
pleasure beyond the satisfaction of any basic physiological need.
It arises from various sources, seeks satisfaction in many different
ways and makes use of many diverse objects for its aim of
achieving pleasure. Only with great difficulty and then never
perfectly does it move from being a drive with many component
parts – a single 'libido' expressed through very different phenomena – to being what is normally understood as sexuality, something which *appears* to be a unified instinct in which genitality
predominates.

For all psychoanalysts the development of the human subject,
its unconscious and its sexuality go hand-in-hand, they are causa-
tively intertwined. A psychoanalyst could not subscribe to a
currently popular sociological distinction in which a person is
born with their biological gender to which society – general
environment, parents, education, the media – adds a socially
defined sex, masculine or feminine. Psychoanalysis cannot make
such a distinction: a person is formed *through* their sexuality, it
could not be 'added' to him or her. The ways in which psychosexuality and the unconscious are closely bound together are
complex, but most obviously, the unconscious contains wishes
that cannot be satisfied and hence have been repressed. Predominant among such wishes are the tabooed incestuous desires
of childhood.

The unconscious contains all that has been repressed from
consciousness, but it is not co-terminous with this. There is an
evident lack of continuity in conscious psychic life – psychoanalysis concerns itself with the gaps. Freud's contribution was
to demonstrate that these gaps constitute a system that is entirely
different from that of consciousness: the unconscious. The unconscious is governed by its own laws, its images do not follow

each other as in the sequential logic of consciousness but by condensing onto each other or by being displaced onto something else. Because it is *unconscious*, direct access to it is impossible but its manifestations are apparent most notably in dreams, everyday slips, jokes, the 'normal' splits and divisions within the human subject and in psychotic and neurotic behaviour.

Lacan believed that though all psychoanalysts subscribe to the importance of the unconscious and to the privileged position of sexuality within the development of the human subject, the way in which many post-Freudians have elaborated their theories ultimately reduces or distorts the significance even of these fundamental postulates. To Lacan most current psychoanalytic thinking is tangled up in popular ideologies and thus misses the revolutionary nature of Freud's work and replicates what it is its task to expose: psychoanalysis should not subscribe to ideas about how men and women do or should live as sexually differentiated beings, but instead it should analyse how they come to be such beings in the first place.

Lacan's work has always to be seen within the context of a two-pronged polemic. Most simply he took on, sometimes by explicit, named reference, more often by indirect insult or implication, almost all analysts of note since Freud. Both internationally and within France, Lacan's history was one of repeated institutional conflict and ceaseless opposition to established views. Outside France his targets were the theories of American dominated ego-psychology, of Melanie Klein and of object-relations analysts,[1] most notably, Balint, Fairbairn and Winnicott. Lacan was more kindly disposed to the clinical insights of some than he was towards those of others but he argued that they are all guilty of misunderstanding and debasing the theory inaugurated by Freud.

1. It is important to keep psychoanalytic object-relations theory distinct from psychological or sociological accounts to which it might bear some superficial resemblance. The 'object' in question is, of course, the human object; but, more importantly, it is its *internalisation* by the subject that is the issue at stake. It is never only an actual object but also always the fantasies of it, that shape it as an internal image for the subject. Object-relations theory originated as an attempt to shift psychoanalysis away from a one-person to a two-person theory stressing that there is always a relationship between at least two people. In object-relations theory the object is active in relation to the subject who is formed in complex interaction with it. This contrasts with Lacan's account of the object, see p. 31 below.

The second prong of Lacan's polemic relates to a mistake he felt Freud himself initiated: paradoxically, while cherishing the wounds of his rejection by a lay and medical public, Freud strove to be easily understood. The preposterous difficulty of Lacan's style is a challenge to easy comprehension, to the popularisation and secularisation of psychoanalysis as it has occurred most notably in North America. Psychoanalysis should aim to show us that we do not know those things we think we do; it therefore cannot assault our popular conceptions by using the very idiom it is intended to confront; a challenge to ideology cannot rest on a linguistic appeal to that same ideology. The dominant ideology of today, as it was of the time and place when psychoanalysis was established, is humanism. Humanism believes that man is at the centre of his own history and of himself; he is a subject more or less in control of his own actions, exercising choice. Humanistic psychoanalytic practice is in danger of seeing the patient as someone who has lost control and a sense of a real or true self (identity) and it aims to help regain these. The matter and manner of all Lacan's work challenges this notion of the human subject: there is none such. In the sentence structure of most of his public addresses and of his written style the grammatical subject is either absent or shifting or, at most, only passively constructed. At this level, the difficulty of Lacan's style could be said to mirror his theory.

The humanistic conception of mankind assumes that the subject exists from the beginning. At least by implication ego psychologists, object-relations theorists and Kleinians base themselves on the same premise. For this reason, Lacan considers that in the last analysis, they are more ideologues than theorists of psychoanalysis. In the Freud that Lacan uses, neither the unconscious nor sexuality can in any degree be pre-given facts, they are constructions; that is they are objects with histories and the human subject itself is only formed within these histories. It is this history of the human subject in its generality (human history) and its particularity (the specific life of the individual) as it manifests itself in unconscious fantasy life, that psychoanalysis traces. This immediately establishes the framework within which the whole question of female sexuality can be understood. As Freud put it: 'In conformity with its peculiar nature, psychoanalysis does not try to describe what a woman is – that would be a task it could scarcely perform – but sets about enquiring *how she comes into being'* (Freud, XXII, 1933, p. 116: italics added).

Lacan dedicated himself to reorienting psychoanalysis to its task of deciphering the ways in which the human subject is constructed – how it comes into being – out of the small human animal. It is because of this aim that Lacan offered psychoanalytic theory the new science of linguistics which he developed and altered in relation to the concept of subjectivity. The human animal is born into language and it is within the terms of language that the human subject is constructed. Language does not arise from within the individual, it is always out there in the world outside, lying in wait for the neonate. Language always 'belongs' to another person. The human subject is created from a general law that comes to it from outside itself and through the speech of other people, though this speech in its turn must relate to the general law.

Lacan's human subject is the obverse of the humanists'. His subject is not an entity with an identity, but a being created in the fissure of a radical split. The identity that seems to be that of the subject is in fact a mirage arising when the subject forms an image of itself by identifying with others' perception of it. When the human baby learns to say 'me' and 'I' it is only acquiring these designations from someone and somewhere else, from the world which perceives and names it. The terms are not constants in harmony with its own body, they do not come from within itself but from elsewhere. Lacan's human subject is not a 'divided self' (Laing) that in a different society could be made whole, but a self which is only actually and necessarily created within a split – a being that can only conceptualise itself when it is mirrored back to itself from the position of another's desire. The unconscious where the subject is not itself, where the 'I' of a dream can be someone else and the object and subject shift and change places, bears perpetual witness to this primordial splitting.

It is here too, within the necessary divisions that language imposes on humans, that sexuality must also find its place. The psychoanalytic notion that sexual wishes are tabooed and hence repressed into the unconscious is frequently understood in a sociological sense (Malinowski, Reich, Marcuse . . .). The implication is that a truly permissive society would not forbid what is now sexually taboo and it would thus liberate men and women from the sense that they are alienated from their own sexuality. But against such prevalent notions, Lacan states that desire itself, and with it, sexual desire, can only exist by virtue of its alienation. Freud describes how the baby can be observed to hallucinate the milk that has been withdrawn from it and the infant to play throwing-away games to overcome the trauma of its mother's necessary departures. Lacan uses these instances to show that the object that is longed for only comes into existence *as an object* when it is lost to the baby or infant. Thus any satisfaction that might subsequently be attained will always contain this loss within it. Lacan refers to this dimension as 'desire'. The baby's need can be met, its demand responded to, but its desire only exists because of the initial failure of satisfaction. Desire persists as an effect of a primordial absence and it therefore indicates that, in this area, there is something fundamentally impossible about satisfaction itself. It is this process that, to Lacan, lies behind Freud's statement that 'We must reckon with the possibility that something in the nature of the sexual instinct itself is unfavourable to the realisation of complete satisfaction' (Freud, XI, 1912, pp. 188–9).

This account of sexual desire led Lacan, as it led Freud, to his adamant rejection of any theory of the difference between the sexes in terms of pre-given male or female entities which complete and satisfy each other. Sexual difference can only be the consequence of a division; without this division it would cease to exist. But it must exist because no human being can become a subject outside the division into two sexes. One must take up a position as either a man or a woman. Such a position is by no means identical with one's biological sexual characteristics, nor is it a position of which one can be very confident – as the psychoanalytical experience demonstrates.

The question as to what created this difference between the sexes was a central debate among psychoanalysts in the twenties and thirties. Lacan returned to this debate as a focal point for what he considered had gone wrong with psychoanalytic theory subsequently. Again Lacan underscored and reformulated the position that Freud took up in this debate. Freud always insisted that it was the presence or absence of the phallus and *nothing else* that marked the distinction between the sexes. Others disagreed. Retrospectively the key concept of the debate becomes transparently clear: it is the castration complex. In Freud's eventual schema, the little boy and the little girl initially share the same sexual history which he terms 'masculine'. They start by desiring their first object: the mother. In fantasy this means having the phallus which is the object of the mother's desire (the phallic phase). This position is forbidden (the castration complex) and the differentiation of the sexes occurs. The castration complex ends the boy's Oedipus complex (his love for his mother) and inaugurates for the girl the one that is specifically hers: she will transfer her object love to her father who seems to have the phallus and identify with her mother who, to the girl's fury, has not. Henceforth the girl will desire to have the phallus and the boy will struggle to represent it. For this reason, for both sexes, this is the insoluble desire of their lives and, for Freud, because its entire point is precisely to be insoluble, it is the bedrock beneath which psychoanalysis cannot reach. Psychoanalysis cannot give the human subject that which it is its fate, as the condition of its subjecthood, to do without:

> At no other point in one's analytic work does one suffer more from an oppressive feeling that all one's repeated efforts have been in vain, and from a suspicion that one has been 'preaching to the winds', than when one is trying to persuade a woman to abandon her wish for a penis on the ground of its being un-realizable. (Freud, XXIII, 1937, p. 252)

There was great opposition to Freud's concept of the girl's phallic phase and to the significance he eventually gave to the castration complex. Lacan returns to the key concept of the debate, to the castration complex and, within its terms, the meaning of the phallus. He takes them as the bedrock of subjectivity itself and of the place of sexuality within it. The selection of the phallus as the mark around which subjectivity and sexuality are constructed reveals, precisely, that they are constructed, in a division which is both arbitrary and alienating. In Lacan's reading of Freud, the threat of castration is not something that has been done to an already existent girl subject or that could be done to an already existent boy subject; it is, as it was for Freud, what 'makes' the girl a girl and the boy a boy, in a division that is both essential and precarious.

The question of the castration complex split psychoanalysts. By the time of the great debate in the mid-twenties, the issue was posed as the nature of female sexuality but underlying that are the preceding disagreements on castration anxiety. In fact all subsequent work on female sexuality and on the construction of sexual difference stems from the various places accorded to the concept of the castration complex. It stands as the often silent centre of all the theories that flourished in the decades before the war; the effects of its acceptance or rejection are still being felt.

The arguments on female sexuality are usually referred to as the 'Freud–Jones debate'. In the presentation that follows I have not adhered to the privileging of Jones's work. This is partly because it is the subject of a detailed examination in one of the texts translated here (P, pp. 99–122); but more importantly because the purpose of my selection is to draw attention to the general nature of the problem and present Freud's work from the perspective to which Lacan returns. I shall leave aside details of differences between analysts; rank those otherwise different on the same side; omit the arguments of any analyst, major or minor, whose contribution in this area does not affect the general proposition – the selection will seem arbitrary from any viewpoint other than this one. Individual authors on the same side differ from one another, are inconsistent with themselves or change their minds, but these factors fade before the more fundamental division around the concept of castration. In the final analysis the debate relates to the question of the psychoanalytic understanding both of sexuality and of the unconscious and brings to the fore issues of the relationship between psychoanalysis and biology and sociology. Is it biology, environmental influence, object-relations or the castration complex that makes for the psychological distinction between the sexes?

Freud, and Lacan after him, are both accused of producing phallocentric theories – of taking man as the norm and woman as what is different therefrom. Freud's opponents are concerned to right the balance and develop theories that explain how men and women in their psychosexuality are equal but different. To both Freud and Lacan their task is not to produce justice but to explain this difference which to them uses, not the man, but the phallus to which the man has to lay claim, as its key term. But it is because Freud's position only clearly became this in his later work that Lacan insists we have to 're-read it', giving his theory the significance and coherence which otherwise it lacks.

Although Lacan takes no note of it, there is, in fact, much in Freud's early work, written long before the great debate, that later analysts could use as a starting-point for their descriptions of the equal, parallel development of the sexes. Divisions within writings on the subject since, in many ways, can be seen in terms of this original divergence within Freud's own work.

Freud's work on this subject can be divided into two periods. In the first phase what he had to say about female sexuality arises in the context of his defence of his theory of the fact and the importance of infantile sexuality in general before a public he considered hostile to his discoveries. This first phase stretches from the 1890s to somewhere between 1916 and 1919. The second phase lasts from 1920 until his final work published post-humously in 1940. In this second period he is concerned with elaborating and defending his understanding of sexuality in relation to the particular question of the nature of the difference between the sexes. By this time what he wrote was part of a discussion within the psychoanalytic movement itself.

In the first phase there is a major contradiction in Freud's work which was never brought out into the open. It was immensely important for the later theories of female sexuality. In this period Freud's few explicit ideas about female sexuality revolve around his references to the Oedipus complex. The essence of the Oedipus complex is first mentioned in his published writings in a passing reference to *Oedipus Rex* in *The Interpretation of Dreams* (1900), in 1910 it is named as the Oedipus complex and by 1919, without much theoretical but with a great deal of clinical expansion (most notably in the case of Little Hans), it has become the foundation stone of psychoanalysis. The particular ways in which the Oedipus complex appears and is resolved characterise different types of normality and pathology; its event and resolution explain the human subject and human desire. But the Oedipus complex of this early period is a simple set of relationships in which the child desires the parent of the opposite sex and feels hostile rivalry for the one of the same sex as itself. There is a symmetrical correspondence in the history of the boy and the girl. Thus in 'Fragment of an Analysis of a Case of Hysteria' (1905) Freud writes: 'Distinct traces are probably to be found in most people of an early partiality of this kind – on the part of a daughter for her father, or on the part of a son for his mother' (Freud, VII, 1905, p. 56), and the entire manifest interpretation of Dora's hysteria is in terms of her infantile Oedipal love for her father, and his substitute in the present, Herr K. Or, in 'Delusions and Dreams in Jensen's *Gradiva*': 'it is the general rule for a normally constituted girl to turn her affection towards her father in the first instance' (Freud, IX, 1906/7, p. 33). And so on. At the root of Freud's assigning parallel Oedipal roles to girls and boys lies a notion of a natural and normative heterosexual attraction; a notion which was to be re-assumed by many psychoanalysts later. Here, in Freud's early work, it is as though the concept of an Oedipus complex – of a fundamental wish for incest – was so radical that if one was to argue at all for the child's incestuous desires then at least these had better be for the parent of the opposite sex. Thus it was because Freud had to defend his thesis of infantile incestuous sexuality so strenuously against both external opposition and his own reluctance to accept the idea, that the very radicalism of the concept of the Oedipus complex acted as a conservative 'stopper' when it came to understanding the difference between the sexes. Here Freud's position is a conventional one: boys will be boys and love women, girls will be girls and love men. Running counter, however, to the normative implications of sexual symmetry in the Oedipal situation are several themes. Most importantly there is both the structure and the argument of the *Three Essays on the Theory of Sexuality* (1905). Lacan returns to this work reading the concept of the sexual drive that he finds latent there through the light shed on it in Freud's later paper on 'Instincts and Their Vicissitudes' (1915).

The *Three Essays* is the revolutionary founding work for the psychoanalytic concept of sexuality. Freud starts the book with chapters on sexual aberration. He uses homosexuality to demonstrate that for the sexual drive there is no natural, automatic object; he uses the perversions to show that it has no fixed aim. As normality is itself an 'ideal fiction' and there is no qualitative distinction between abnormality and normality, innate factors cannot account for the situation and any notion of the drive as simply innate is therefore untenable. What this means is that the understanding of the drive itself is at stake. The drive (or 'instinct' in the Standard Edition translation), is something on the border between the mental and the physical. Later Freud formulated the relationship as one in which the somatic urge delegated its task to a psychical representative. In his paper, 'The Unconscious', he wrote:

An instinct can never become an object of consciousness – only the idea that represents the instinct can. Even in the unconscious, moreover, an instinct cannot be represented otherwise than by an idea . . . . When we nevertheless speak of an unconscious instinctual impulse or of a repressed instinctual impulse . . . we can only mean an instinctual impulse the ideational representative of which is unconscious. (Freud, XIV, 1915, p. 177)

There is never a causal relationship between the biological urge and its representative: we cannot perceive an activity and deduce behind it a corresponding physical motive force. The sexual drive is never an entity, it is polymorphous, its aim is variable, its object contingent. Lacan argues that the *Three Essays* demonstrate that Freud was already aware that for mankind the drive is almost the *opposite* of an animal instinct that knows and gets its satisfying object. On the other hand, object-relations theorists contend that Freud suggested that the sexual drive was a direct outgrowth of the first satisfying relationship with the mother; it repeats the wish to suck or be held. The baby thus has a first 'part-object' in the breast and later an object in the mother whom it will love pre-Oedipally and then as a 'whole object' Oedipally. Later the sexual drive of the adult will seek out a substitute for this which, if it is good enough, can and will satisfy it.

Though the lack of clarity in some parts of the *Three Essays* could, perhaps, be held responsible for this diversity of interpretation and for the new dominant strand of humanism that Lacan deplores, yet there is absolutely nothing within the essays that is compatible with any notion of natural heterosexual attraction or with the Oedipus complex as it is formulated in Freud's other writing of this period. The structure and content of the *Three Essays* erodes any idea of normative sexuality. By deduction, if no heterosexual attraction is ordained in nature, there can be no genderised sex – there cannot at the outset be a male or female person in a psychological sense.

In the case of 'Dora', Freud assumed that had Dora not been an hysteric she would have been naturally attracted to her suitor, Herr K, just as she had been attracted to her father when she was a small child. In other words, she would have had a natural female Oedipus complex. But the footnotes, written subsequently, tell another story: Dora's relationship to her father had been one not only of attraction but also of identification with him. In terms of her sexual desire, Dora is a man adoring a woman. To ascribe the situation to Dora's hysteria would be to beg the whole founding question of psychoanalysis. Hysteria is not produced by any innate disposition. It follows that if Dora can have a masculine identification there can be no natural or automatic heterosexual drive.

Until the 1920s Freud solved this problem by his notion of bisexuality. 'Bisexuality' likewise enabled him to avoid what would otherwise have been too blatant a contradiction in his position: thus he argued that the too neat parallelism of the boy's and girl's Oedipal situations, the dilemma of Dora, the presence of homosexuality, could all be accounted for by the fact that the boy has a bit of the female, the girl of the male. This saves the Oedipus complex from the crudity of gender determinism – but at a price. If, as Freud insists, the notion of bisexuality is not to be a purely biological one, whence does it arise? Later analysts who largely preserved Freud's early use of the term, did relate bisexuality to the duplications of anatomy or based it on simple identification: the boy partly identified with the mother, the girl partly with the father. For Freud, when later he reformulated the Oedipus complex, 'bisexuality' shifted its meaning and came to stand for the very uncertainty of sexual division itself.

Without question during this first period, Freud's position is highly contradictory. His discovery of the Oedipus complex led him to assume a natural heterosexuality. The rest of his work argued against this possibility as the very premise of a psycho-analytic understanding of sexuality. There is no reference to the Oedipus complex or the positions it assumes in the *Three Essays* and by this omission he was able to avoid recognising the contradiction within his theses, though the essays bear its mark within some of the confusing statements they contain.

By about 1915 it seems that Freud was aware that his theory of the Oedipus complex and of the nature of sexuality could not satisfactorily explain the difference between the sexes. Freud never explicitly stated his difficulties (as he did in other areas of work), but in 1915, he added a series of footnotes to the *Three Essays* which are almost all about the problem of defining masculinity and femininity. Other writers – notably Jung – had taken Freud's ideas on the Oedipus complex as they were expressed at the time, to their logical conclusion and in establishing a definite parity between the sexes had re-named the girl's Oedipal conflict, the Electra complex. Whether or not it was this work – Freud rejected the Electra complex from the outset – or whether it was the dawning awareness of the unsatisfactory nature of his own position that provoked Freud to re-think the issue cannot be established; but something made him look more intensively at the question of the difference between the sexes.

One concept, also added in 1915 to the *Three Essays*, marks both the turning point in Freud's own understanding of the differences between men and women, and also the focal point of the conflict that emerges between his views and those of most other analysts on the question. This concept is the castration complex.

During the first phase of Freud's work we can see the idea of the castration complex gradually gain momentum. It was discussed in 'On the Sexual Theories of Children' (1908), crucially important in the analysis of Little Hans (1909), yet when he wrote 'On Narcissism: An Introduction' in 1914 Freud was still uncertain as to whether or not it was a universal occurrence. But in 1915 it starts to assume a larger and larger part. By 1924, in the paper on 'The Dissolution of the Oedipus Complex' the castration complex has emerged as a central concept. In his autobiography of 1925, Freud wrote: 'The *castration complex* is of the profoundest importance in the formation alike of character and of neurosis' (Freud, xx, 1925, p. 37). He made it the focal point of the acquisition of culture; it operates as a law whereby men and women assume their humanity and, inextricably bound up with this, it gives the human meaning of the distinction between the sexes.

The castration complex in Freud's writings is very closely connected with his interest in man's prehistory. It is unnecessary to enumerate Freud's dubious anthropological reconstructions in this field; what is of relevance is the importance he gave to an *event* in man's personal and social history. It is well known that before he recognised the significance of fantasy and of infantile sexuality, Freud believed the tales his hysterical patients told him of their seductions by their fathers. Although Freud abandoned the particular event of paternal seduction as either likely or, more important, causative, he retained the notion of an event, pre-historical or actual. Something intruded from without into the child's world. Something that was not innate but came from outside, from history or prehistory. This 'event' was to be the paternal threat of castration.

That the castration complex operates as an external event, a law, can be seen too from a related preoccupation of Freud's. Some time around 1916, Freud became interested in the ideas of Lamarck. This interest is most often regarded, with condescension, as an instance of Freud's nineteenth-century scientific anachronism. But in fact by 1916 Lamarck was already outmoded and it is clear that Freud's interest arose not from ignorance but from the need to account for something that he observed but could not theorise. The question at stake was: how does the individual acquire the whole essential history of being human within the first few short years of its life? Lamarckian notions of cultural inheritance offered Freud a possible solution to the problem. In rejecting the idea of cultural inheritance, Freud's opponents may have been refusing a false solution but in doing so they missed the urgency of the question and thereby failed to confront the problem of how the child acquires so early and so rapidly its knowledge of human law. Karen Horney's 'culturalist' stress – her emphasis on the influence of society – was an attempt to put things right, but it failed because it necessitated an implicit assumption that the human subject could be set apart from society and was not constructed solely within it: the child and society were separate entities mutually affecting each other. For Horney there are men and women (boys and girls) already there; in this she takes for granted exactly that which she intends to explain.

Freud's concept of the castration complex completely shifted the implications of the Oedipus complex and altered the meaning of bisexuality. Before the castration complex was given its full significance, it seems that the Oedipus complex dissolved naturally, a passing developmental stage. Once the castration complex is postulated it is this alone that shatters the Oedipus complex. The castration complex institutes the superego as its representative and as representative thereby of the law. Together with the organising role of the Oedipus complex in relation to desire, the castration complex governs the position of each person in the triangle of father, mother and child; in the way it does this, it embodies the law that founds the human order itself. Thus the question of castration, of sexual difference as the product of a division, and the concept of an historical and symbolic order, all begin, tentatively, to come together. It is on their interdependence that Lacan bases his theories in the texts that follow.

When Freud started to elevate the concept of castration to its theoretical heights, resistance started. It seems that infantile sexuality and the Oedipus complex were unpalatable ideas for many outside the psychoanalytical movement, yet it would appear that there was something even more inherently unacceptable about the notion of a castration complex and what it assumed in the girl child, penis envy, even for psychoanalysts. After this point, Freud's emphasis on the importance of the castration complex comes not only from his clinical observations, his growing awareness of the contradictions of his own work, his increasing interest in the foundations of human history, but to a degree as a response to the work of his colleagues.

Lou Andreas-Salomé, van Ophuijsen, then Karl Abraham and Auguste Starcke in 1921 initiate the response to the notion. Franz Alexander, Otto Rank, Carl Müller-Braunschweig, and Josine Müller continue it until the names that are more famous in this context – Karen Horney, Melanie Klein, Lampl-de Groot, Helene Deutsch, Ernest Jones – are added in the mid-twenties and thirties. Others join in: Fenichel, Rado, Marjorie Brierley, Joan Rivière, Ruth Mack Brunswick, but by 1935 the positions have clarified and the terms of the discussion on sexual differences do not change importantly, though the content that goes to fill out the argument does so.

Karl Abraham's work is crucial. He died before the great debate was in full flow, but his ideas, though often not acknowledged, were central to it – not least because most of Freud's opponents believed that Abraham's views were representative of Freud's. As Abraham is ostensibly amplifying Freud's work and writing in support of the concept of the castration complex, this was an understandable but completely mistaken assumption. In their letters Freud and Abraham are always agreeing most politely with one another and this makes it rather hard to elucidate the highly significant differences between them. One difference is that Freud argues that girls envy the phallus, Karl Abraham believes that both sexes in parallel fashion fear castration – which he describes as lack of sexual potency.[2] In

2. This difference was to be taken further by other writers, most notably by Ernest Jones who in arguing against the specificity of phallic castration and for the general fear of an extinction of sexual desire, coined the term

Abraham's thesis, boys and girls – because they are already different – respond differently to an identical experience; in Freud the same experience distinguishes them. By implication for Abraham, but not for Freud, by the time of the castration complex there must already be 'boys' and 'girls'. This important distinction apart, the real divergence between Abraham's arguments and those of Freud can best be glimpsed through the shift of emphasis. In the work of both writers incest is taboo ('castration'); but only for Freud must there be someone around to forbid it: prohibition is in the air.

In Freud's work, with its emphasis on the castration complex as the source of the law, it is the father who already possesses the mother, who metaphorically says 'no' to the child's desires. The prohibition only comes to be meaningful to the child because there are people – females – who have been castrated in the particular sense that they are without the phallus. It is only, in other words, through 'deferred action' that previous experiences such as the sight of female genitals become significant. Thus, for Freud, contained within the very notion of the castration complex is the theory that other experiences and perceptions only take their meaning from the law for which it stands. In Abraham's work, to the contrary, the threat of castration arises from an actual perception that the child makes about a girl's body: no one intervenes, there is no prohibiting father whose threat is the utterance of a law; here it is the 'real' inferiority of the female genitals that once comprehended initiates the complex in both sexes.

Here, however, within Freud's work, we come across a further and most important contradiction; it was one he did not have time fully to resolve. It is a contradiction that explains subsequent readings of Abraham's and Freud's work as co-incident. Freud is clear that the boy's castration complex arises

---

aphanisis to cover his idea. This notion is not developed in Abraham's work but it did, however, set a future trend. Lacan returns to it, arguing that Jones so nearly hit the mark that his failure is the more grotesque for his near-insight. To Lacan, *aphanisis* relates to the essential division of the subject whereas, he writes, Jones 'mistook it for something rather absurd, the fear of seeing desire disappear. Now *aphanisis* is to be situated in a more radical way at the level at which the subject manifests himself in this movement I describe as lethal. In a quite different way, I have called this movement the *fading* of the subject.' 'The subject appears on the one side as meaning and on the other as *fading* – disappearance (SXI, pp. 189, 199, *pp. 207–8, 218*).

from the penis being given significance from the father's prohibition; but sometimes he suggests that the girl's penis envy comes from a simple perception that she makes; she sees the actual penis, realises it is bigger and better and wants one. Clearly such inequity in girls' and boys' access to meaning is untenable: why should the girl have a privileged relationship to an understanding of the body? In fact there is evidence that Freud was aware of the discrepancy in his account; his published statements tend to be confusing, but in a letter he wrote: 'the sight of the penis and its function of urination cannot be the motive, only the trigger of the child's envy. However, no one has stated this' (Freud, 1935, 1971, p. 329). Unfortunately neither Freud nor any subsequent analyst stated this clearly enough in their published writings.

Freud referred to Abraham's article on the female castration complex (1920) as 'unsurpassed'. But absolutely nothing in the theoretical framework of Freud's writing confirmed Abraham's perspective. Freud certainly talks of the woman's sense of 'organ-inferiority' but this is never for him the *motive* for the castration complex or hence for the dissolution of the Oedipus complex; it is therefore not causative of female sexuality, femininity or neurosis. For Freud the absence of the penis in women is significant only in that it makes meaningful the father's prohibition on incestuous desires. In and of itself, the female body neither indicates nor initiates anything. The implication of the different stress of Freud and Abraham is very far-reaching. If, as in Abraham's work, the actual body is seen as a motive for the constitution of the subject in its male or female sexuality, then an historical or symbolic dimension to this constitution is precluded. Freud's intention was to establish that very dimension as the *sine qua non* of the construction of the human subject. It is on this dimension that Lacan bases his entire account of sexual difference.

If Freud considered that the actual body of the child on its own was irrelevant to the castration complex, so too did he repeatedly urge that the actual situation of the child, the presence or absence of the father, the real prohibition against masturbation and so on, could be insignificant compared with the ineffable presence of a symbolic threat (the 'event') to which one is inevitably subjected as the price of being human. Unable to accept the notion of cultural inheritance, other analysts, agreeing with Freud that an actual occurrence could not account for the omnipresent castration anxiety they found in their clinical work, had to look elsewhere for an explanation. In all cases, they considered the castration complex not as something essential to the very construction of the human subject but as a fear that arises from the internal experiences of a being who is already, even if only in a primitive form, constituted as a subject. As a consequence, in none of these alternative theories can castration have any fundamental bearing on sexual difference.

Thus Starcke found the prevalence of castration anxiety in the loss of the nipple from the baby's mouth, so that daily weaning accounted for the universality of the complex. As a further instance he proposed the baby's gradual ability to see itself as distinct from the external world: 'The formation of the outer world is the original castration; the withdrawal of the nipple forms the root-conception of this' (Starcke, 1921, p. 180). Franz Alexander and Otto Rank took castration back to the baby's loss of the womb, which was once part of itself. Freud took up his colleague's ideas on separation anxiety (as he termed it) most fully in *Inhibitions, Symptoms and Anxiety* written in 1925, but two years earlier he had added this footnote to the case of Little Hans:

> While recognizing all of these roots of the complex, I have nevertheless put forward the view that the term 'castration complex' ought to be confined to those excitations and consequences which are bound up with the loss of the *penis*. Any one who, in analysing adults, has become convinced of the invariable presence of the castration complex, will of course find difficulty in ascribing its origin to a chance threat – of a kind which is not, after all, of such universal occurrence; he will be driven to assume that children construct this danger for themselves out of the slightest hints . . . (Freud, x, 1909, p. 8, n[2], 1923)

There is a fundamental distinction between recognising that the castration complex may refer back to other separations and actually seeing these separations as castrations. To Freud the castration complex divided the sexes and thus made the human being, human. But this is not to deny the importance of earlier separations. Freud himself had proposed that the loss of the faeces constituted the possibility of a retrospective referral; the castration complex could use it as a model. Freud's account is retroactive: fearing phallic castration the child may 'recollect' previous losses, castration gives them their relevance. In the other accounts it is these separations that make castration relevant; here the scheme is prospective: early losses make the child fear future ones. For Freud, history and the psychoanalytic experience is always a reconstruction, a retrospective account: the human subject is part of such a history. The other explanations make him grow developmentally. If one takes castration itself back to the womb, then the human subject was there from the outset and it can only follow that what makes him psychotic, neurotic or 'normal' is some arbitrarily selected constitutional factor or some equally arbitrary environmental experience.

Once more, Lacan underlines and reformulates Freud's position. The castration complex is *the* instance of the humanisation of the child in its sexual difference. Certainly it rejoins other severances, in fact it gives them their meaning. If the specific mark of the phallus, the repression of which is the institution of the law, is repudiated then there can only be psychosis. To Lacan all other hypotheses make nonsense of psychoanalysis. For him they once again leave unanswered the question whence the subject originates, and, he asks, what has happened to the language and social order that distinguishes him or her from other mammals – is it to have no effect other than a subsidiary one, on formation? Above all, how can sexual difference be understood within such a developmental perspective?

If it is argued that there is nothing specific about the threat of phallic castration; if birth, weaning, the formation of the outer world are all castrations, then something else has to explain the difference between the sexes. If castration is only one among other separations or is the same as the dread of the loss of sexual desire common to men and women alike (Jones's *aphanisis*), then what distinguishes the two sexes? All the major contributors to this field at this period, whether they supplemented or opposed Freud, found the explanation in a biological predisposition. This is the case with Freud's biologistic defender, Helene Deutsch, as it is with his culturalist opponent, Karen Horney.

The demoting of the castration complex from its key role in the construction of sexual difference, and the subsequent reliance on biological explanations, was accompanied by a further change. In the mid-twenties the focus of discussion shifted and a new epoch began. The crisis of the concept of the castration complex may well have contributed to a change of emphasis away from itself and towards a preoccupation with female sexuality. When the well-known names associated with the discussion – Horney, Deutsch, Lampl-de Groot, Klein, Jones – join in, their concern is less with the construction of sexual difference than it is with the nature of female sexuality. It is from this time that we can date what has become known as the 'great debate'. The debate was to reach its peak when in 1935, Ernest Jones, invited to Vienna to give some lectures to elucidate the fast growing differences between British and Viennese psycho-analysts, chose as his first (and, as it turned out, only) topic, female sexuality. While female sexuality of course is central to our concerns, we can see that something highly important was lost in the change of emphasis. Retrospectively one can perceive that the reference point is still the distinction between the sexes (the point of the castration complex) but by concentrating on the status and nature of female sexuality, it often happens that this is treated as an isolate, something independent of the distinction that creates it. This tendency is confirmed within the theories of those opposed to Freud. The opposition to Freud saw the con-cept of the castration complex as derogatory to women. In repudiating its terms they hoped both to elevate women and to explain what women consisted of – a task Freud ruled as psycho-analytically out-of-bounds. But from now on analysts who came in on Freud's side also saw their work in this way. Women, so to speak, had to have something of their own. The issue subtly shifts from what distinguishes the sexes to what has each sex got of value that belongs to it alone. In this context, and in the absence of the determining role of the castration complex, it is inevitable that there is a return to the very biological explanations from which Freud deliberately took his departure – where else could that something else be found?

For Freud it is of course never a question of arguing that anatomy or biology is irrelevant, it is a question of assigning them their place. He gave them a place – it was outside the field of psychoanalytic enquiry. Others put them firmly within it. Thus Carl Müller-Braunschweig, assuming, as did others, that there was an innate masculinity and femininity which corresponded directly with the biological male and female, wrote of a 'masculine and feminine id'. There is now not only an original masculinity and femininity but a natural heterosexuality. In 1926, Karen Horney spoke of the 'biological principle of heterosexual attraction' and argued from this that the girl's so-called masculine phase is a defence against her primary feminine anxiety that her father will violate her. Melanie Klein elaborated the increasingly prevalent notion that because of her primordial infantile feminine sexuality, the girl has an unconscious knowledge of the vagina. This naturalist perspective, exemplified in the work of Ernest Jones, posits a primary femininity for the girl based on her biological sex which then suffers vicissitudes as a result of fantasies brought into play by the girl's relations to objects. The theorists of this position do not deny Freud's notion that the girl has a phallic phase, but they argue that it is only a reaction-formation against her natural feminine attitude. It is a secondary formation, a temporary state in which the girl takes refuge when she feels her femininity is in danger. Just as the boy with his natural male valuation of his penis fears its castration, so the girl with her natural femininity will fear the destruction of her insides through her father's rape. The presence or absence of early vaginal sensations becomes a crucial issue in this context – a context in which impulses themselves, in a direct and unmediated way, produce psychological characteristics. Freud argued strenuously against such a position. In a letter that, read in this context, is not as cryptic as it at first appears, he wrote to Müller-Braunschweig:

> I object to all of you (Horney, Jones, Rado, etc.,) to the extent that you do not distinguish more clearly and cleanly between what is psychic and what is biological, that you try to establish a neat parallelism between the two and that you, motivated by such intent, unthinkingly construe psychic facts which are unprovable and that you, in the process of doing so, must declare as reactive or regressive much that without doubt is primary. Of course, these reproaches must remain obscure. In addition, I would only like to emphasize that we must keep psychoanalysis separate from biology just as we have kept it separate from anatomy and physiology . . . (Freud, 1935, 1971, p. 329) . . .

However, there were those opponents of Freud's position who did not want to lean too heavily or too explicitly on a biological explanation of sexual difference; instead they stressed the significance of the psychological mechanism of identification with its dependence on an object. In both Freud's account and those of these object-relations theorists, after the resolution of the Oedipus complex, each child hopefully identifies with the parent of the appropriate sex. The explanations look similar – but the place accorded to the castration complex pushes them poles apart. In Freud's schema, after the castration complex, boys and girls will more or less adequately adopt the sexual identity of the appropriate parent. But it is always only an adoption and a precarious one at that, as long ago, Dora's 'inappropriate' paternal identification had proved. For Freud, identification with the appropriate parent is a *result* of the castration complex which has already given the mark of sexual distinction. For other analysts, dispensing with the key role of the castration complex, identification (with a biological prop) is the *cause* of sexual difference. Put somewhat reductively, the position of these theorists can be elucidated thus: there is a period when the girl is undifferentiated from the boy (for Klein and some others, this is the boy's primary feminine phase) and hence both love and identify with their first object, the mother; then, as a result of her biological sex (her femininity) and because her love has been frustrated on account of her biological inadequacy (she has not got the phallus for her mother and never will have), the little girl enters into her own Oedipus complex and loves her father; she then fully re-identifies with her mother and achieves her full feminine identity.

It can be seen from this that the question of female sexuality was itself crucial in the development of object-relations theory. This understanding of femininity put a heavy stress on the first maternal relationship; the same emphasis has likewise characterised the whole subsequent expansion of object-relations theory. When the 'great debate' evaporated, object-relations theorists concentrated attention on the mother and the sexually undifferentiated child, leaving the problem of sexual distinction as a subsidiary that is somehow not bound up with the very formation of the subject. This is the price paid for the reorientation to the mother, and the neglect of the father, whose prohibition in Freud's theory, alone can represent the mark that distinguishes boys and girls. The mother herself in these accounts has inherited a great deal of the earlier interest in female sexuality – her own experiences, the experiences of her, have been well documented, but she is already constituted – in all her uncertainty – as a female subject. This represents an interesting avoidance of the question of sexual difference.

Freud acknowledged his serious inadequacies in the area of the mother–child relationship. In fact his blindness was dictated not so much by his personal inclinations or his own masculinity – as he and others suggested – but by the nature of psychoanalysis as he conceived it. To Freud, if psychoanalysis is phallocentric, it is because the human social order that it perceives refracted through the individual human subject is patrocentric. To date, the father stands in the position of the third term that *must* break the asocial dyadic unit of mother and child. We can see that this third term will always need to be represented by something or someone. Lacan returns to the problem, arguing that the relation of mother and child cannot be viewed outside the structure established by the position of the father. To Lacan, a theory that ignores the father or sees him embodied within the mother (Klein) or through her eyes, is nonsense. There can be nothing *human* that pre-exists or exists outside the law represented by the father; there is only either its denial (psychosis) or the fortunes and misfortunes ('normality' and neurosis) of its terms. Ultimately for Kleinian and non-Kleinian object-relations theorists (despite the great differences between them) the distinction between the sexes is not the result of a division but a fact that is already given; men and women, males and females, *exist*. There is no surprise here.

The debate with his colleagues also led Freud himself to make some crucial reformulations. Again these can be said to stem from his stress on the castration complex. Time and again in the last papers of his life he underscored its significance. In re-thinking his belief that the boy and the girl both had a phallic phase that was primary, and not, as others argued, reactive and secondary, he re-emphasised, but more importantly, reformulated his earlier positions. The Oedipus complex as he had originally conceived it led to what he considered the impasses and mistakes of the arguments he opposed. The natural heterosexuality it assumed was untenable but its simple reversal with its stress on the first maternal relation was equally unsatisfactory.

Without an ultimate reliance on a biologically induced identificatory premise, such a position does not account for the
difference between the boy and the girl. Lacan would argue that
it is at this juncture that Freud – his earlier positions now seen to
be leading in false directions – brings forward the concept of
desire. 'What', asks Freud, 'does the woman [the little girl]
want?' All answers to the question, including 'the mother' are
false: she simply *wants*. The phallus – with its status as potentially
absent – comes to stand in for the necessarily *missing* object of
desire at the level of sexual division. If this is so, the Oedipus
complex can no longer be a static myth that reflects the real
situation of father, mother and child, it becomes a structure
revolving around the question of where a person can be placed in
relation to his or her desire. That 'where' is determined by the
castration complex.

In his 1933 essay 'Femininity', Freud puts forward the solu-
tions of his opponents on the issue of female sexuality as a series
of questions. He asks 'how does [the little girl] pass from her
masculine phase to the feminine one to which she is biologically
destined?' (Freud, XXII, 1933, p. 119) and contrary to the answers
of his opponents, he concludes that: 'the constitution will not
adapt itself to its function without a struggle' (Freud, XXII, 1933,
p. 117) and that though 'It would be a solution of ideal simplicity
if we could suppose that from a particular age onwards the
elementary influence of the mutual attraction between the sexes
makes itself felt and impels the small woman towards men . . . we
are not going to find things so easy . . .' (Freud, XXII, 1933,
p. 119). The biological female is destined to become a woman,
but the question to which psychoanalysis must address itself, is
how, if she does manage this, is it to happen? His colleagues'
excellent work on the earliest maternal relationship, from a
psychoanalytic point of view, leaves unanswered the problem of
sexual differentiation. As Freud puts it: 'Unless we can find
something that is specific for girls and is not present or not in the
same way present in boys, we shall not have explained the ter-
mination of the attachment of girls to their mother. I believe we
have found this specific factor . . . in the castration complex'
(Freud, 1933, p. 124).

Freud ended his life with an unfinished paper: 'Splitting of the
Ego in the Process of Defence' (XXIII, 1940). It is about the castration complex and its implication for the construction of the

subject. It describes the formation of the ego in a moment of danger (of threatened loss) which results in a primary split from which it never recovers. Freud offers the reaction to the castration complex when a fetish is set up as its alternative, as an exemplary instance of this split. In this paper we can see clearly the position of Freud's to which Lacan is to return. A primordially split subject necessitates an originally lost object. Though Freud does not talk of the object as a lost object as Lacan does, he is absolutely clear that its psychological significance arises from its absence, or as he put it in the essay on 'Femininity' from the fact that it could never satisfy: '. . . the child's avidity for its earliest nourishment is altogether insatiable . . . it never gets over the pain of losing its mother's breast' (Freud, xxii, 1933, p. 122). Even the tribal child, breastfed well beyond infancy, is unsatisfied: pain and lack of satisfaction are the point, the triggers that evoke desire.

Freud's final writings are often perceived as reflecting an old man's despair. But for Lacan their pessimism indicates a clarification and summation of a theory whose implications are and must be, anti-humanist. The issue of female sexuality always brings us back to the question of how the human subject is constituted. In the theories of Freud that Lacan redeploys, the distinction between the sexes brought about by the castration complex and the different positions that must subsequently be taken up, confirms that the subject is split and the object is lost. This is the difficulty at the heart of being human to which psychoanalysis and the objects of its enquiry – the unconscious and sexuality – bear witness. To Lacan, a humanist position offers only false hopes on the basis of false theories.

It is a matter of perspective – and Lacan would argue that the perspective of post-Freudian analysts is ideological in that it confirms the humanism of our times. In the view of Kleinians and other object-relations theorists, whether it is with a primitive ego or as an initial fusion with the mother from which differentiation gradually occurs, the perspective starts from an identification with what seems to be, or ought to be, the subject. The problem these theorists address is: what does the baby/person do with its world in order for it to develop? Then the question is inverted: has the human environment been good enough for the baby to be able to do the right things? In these accounts a sexual identity is first given biologically and then developed and confirmed (or not) as the subject grows through interaction with the real objects and its fantasies of them, on its complicated road to maturity.

Lacan takes the opposite perspective: the analysand's unconscious reveals a fragmented subject of shifting and uncertain sexual identity. To be human is to be subjected to a law which de-centres and divides: sexuality is created in a division, the subject is split; but an ideological world conceals this from the conscious subject who is supposed to feel whole and certain of a sexual identity. Psychoanalysis should aim at a destruction of this concealment and at a reconstruction of the subject's construction in all its splits. This may be an accurate theory, it is certainly a precarious project. It is to this theory and project – the history of the fractured sexual subject – that Lacan dedicates himself.

INTRODUCTION – II
Jacqueline Rose

> Freud argues that there is no libido other than masculine. Meaning what? other than that a whole field, which is hardly negligible, is thereby ignored. This is the field of all those beings who take on the status of the woman – if, indeed, this being takes on anything whatsoever of her fate.
>
> (Lacan, Encore, SXX, 1972–3)

The texts we publish here return to and extend the debate which has just been described. They return to it by insisting that its implications for psychoanalysis have still not been understood; they extend it in so far as the issue itself – the question of feminine sexuality – goes beyond psychoanalysis to feminism, as part of its questioning of how that sexuality comes to be defined.

In this sense, these texts bear all the signs of a repetition, a resurfacing of an area of disagreement or disturbance, but one in which the issue at stake has been thrown into starker relief. It is as if the more or less peaceful co-existence which closed the debate of the 1920s and 1930s ('left, in a tacit understanding, to the goodwill of individual interpretation', C, pp. 88–9), and the lull which it produced ('the lull experienced after the breakdown of the debate', C, p. 89), concealed a trouble which was bound to emerge again with renewed urgency. Today, that urgency can be seen explicitly as political, so much so that in the controversy over Lacan's dissolution of his school in 1980, the French newspaper *Le Monde* could point to the debate about femininity as the clearest statement of the political repercussions of psychoanalysis itself (*Le Monde*, 1 June 1980, p. xvi). Psychoanalysis is now recognised as crucial in the discussion of femininity – how it comes into being and what it might mean. Jacques Lacan, who addressed this issue increasingly during the course of his work, has been at the centre of the controversies produced by that recognition.

In this context, the idea of a 'return to Freud' most commonly associated with Lacan has a very specific meaning. It is not so much a return to the letter of Freud's text as the re-opening of a case, a case which has already been fought, as Juliet Mitchell describes above, and one which, if anything, in relation to feminism, Freud could be said to have lost. In fact the relationship between psychoanalysis and feminism might seem to start at the point where Freud's account of sexual difference was rejected by analysts specifically arguing *for* women ('men analysts have been led to adopt an unduly phallo-centric view', Jones, 1927, p. 459). Most analysts have since agreed on the limitations and difficulties of Freud's account. Those difficulties were fully recognised by Lacan, but he considered that attempts to resolve them within psychoanalysis had systematically fallen into a trap. For they failed to see that the concept of the phallus in Freud's account of human sexuality was part of his awareness of the problematic, if not impossible, nature of sexual identity itself. They answered it, therefore, by reference to a pre-given sexual difference aimed at securing that identity for both sexes. In doing so, they lost sight of Freud's sense that sexual difference is constructed at a price and that it involves subjection to a law which exceeds any natural or biological division. The concept of the phallus stands for that subjection, and for the way in which women are very precisely implicated in its process.

The history of psychoanalysis can in many ways be seen entirely in terms of its engagement with this question of feminine sexuality. Freud himself started with the analysis of the hysterical patient (Freud and Breuer, II, 1893–5) (whom, it should be noted, he insisted could also be male (Freud, I, 1886)). It was then his failure to analyse one such patient – 'Dora' (Freud, VII, 1905) – in terms of a normative concept of what a woman should be, or want, that led him to recognise the fragmented and aberrant nature of sexuality itself. Normal sexuality is, therefore, strictly an *ordering*, one which the hysteric refuses (falls ill). The rest of Freud's work can then be read as a description of how that ordering takes place, which led him back, necessarily, to the question of femininity, because its persistence as a difficulty revealed the cost of that order.

Moreover, Freud returned to this question at the moment when he was reformulating his theory of human subjectivity. Lacan took Freud's concept of the unconscious, as extended and developed by the later texts (specifically *Beyond the Pleasure*

Principle, XVIII, 1920, and the unfinished paper 'Splitting of the Ego in the Process of Defence', XXIII, 1940) as the basis of his own account of femininity (the frequent criticism of Lacan that he disregarded the later works is totally unfounded here). He argued that failure to recognise the interdependency of these two concerns in Freud's work – the theory of subjectivity and femininity together – has led psychoanalysts into an ideologically loaded mistake, that is, an attempt to resolve the difficulties of Freud's account of femininity by aiming to resolve the difficulty of femininity itself. For by restoring the woman to her place and identity (which, they argue, Freud out of 'prejudice' failed to see), they have missed Freud's corresponding stress on the division and precariousness of human subjectivity itself, which was, for Lacan, central to psychoanalysis' most radical insights. Attempts by and for women to answer Freud have tended to relinquish those insights, discarding either the concept of the unconscious (the sign of that division) or that of bisexuality (the sign of that precariousness). And this has been true of positions as diverse as that of Jones (and Horney) in the 1920s and 1930s and that of Nancy Chodorow (1979)[1] speaking from psychoanalysis for feminism today.

Re-opening the debate on feminine sexuality must start, therefore, with the link between sexuality and the unconscious. No account of Lacan's work which attempts to separate the two can make sense. For Lacan, the unconscious undermines the subject from any position of certainty, from any relation of knowledge to his or her psychic processes and history, and *simultaneously* reveals the fictional nature of the sexual category to which every human subject is none the less assigned. In Lacan's account, sexual identity operates as a law – it is something enjoined on the subject. For him, the fact that individuals must line up according to an opposition (having or not having the phallus) makes that clear. But it is the constant difficulty, or even impossibility, of that process which Lacan emphasised, and which each of the texts in this collection in differing ways seeks to address. Exposure of that difficulty within psychoanalysis and for feminism is, therefore, part of one and the same project.

1. See Note 4, p. 37 below.

I

The link between sexuality and the unconscious is one that was constantly stressed by Lacan: 'we should not overlook the fact that sexuality is crucially underlined by Freud as being strictly consubstantial to the dimension of the unconscious' (SXI, p. 133, *p. 146*). Other accounts, such as that of Ernest Jones, described the acquisition of sexual identity in terms of ego development and/or the maturation of the drives. Lacan considered that each of these concepts rests on the myth of a subjective cohesion which the concept of the unconscious properly subverts. For Lacan, the description of sexuality in developmental terms invariably loses sight of Freud's most fundamental discovery – that the unconscious never ceases to challenge our apparent identity as subjects.

Lacan's account of subjectivity was always developed with reference to the idea of a fiction. Thus, in the 1930s he introduced the concept of the 'mirror stage' (*Ecrits*, (1936)), which took the child's mirror image as the model and basis for its future identifications. This image is a fiction because it conceals, or freezes, the infant's lack of motor co-ordination and the fragmentation of its drives. But it is salutary for the child, since it gives it the first sense of a coherent identity in which it can recognise itself. For Lacan, however, this is already a fantasy – the very image which places the child divides its identity into two. Furthermore, that moment only has meaning in relation to the presence and the look of the mother who guarantees its reality for the child. The mother does not (as in D. W. Winnicott's account (Winnicott, 1967)) mirror the child to itself; she grants an image *to* the child, which her presence instantly deflects. Holding the child is, therefore, to be understood not only as a containing, but as a process of referring, which fractures the unity it seems to offer. The mirror image is central to Lacan's account of subjectivity, because its apparent smoothness and totality is a myth. The image in which we first recognise ourselves is a *misrecognition*. Lacan is careful to stress, however, that his point is not restricted to the field of the visible alone: 'the idea of the mirror should be understood as an object which reflects – not just the visible, but also what is heard, touched and willed by the child' (Lacan, 1949, p. 567).

Lacan then takes the mirror image as the model of the ego

function itself, the category which enables the subject to operate as 'I'. He supports his argument from linguistics, which designates the pronoun as a 'shifter' (Benveniste, 1956). The 'I' with which we speak stands for our identity as subjects in language, but it is the least stable entity in language, since its meaning is purely a function of the moment of utterance. The 'I' can shift, and change places, because it only ever refers to whoever happens to be using it at the time.

For Lacan the subject is constituted through language – the mirror image represents the moment when the subject is located in an order outside itself to which it will henceforth refer. The subject is the subject *of* speech (Lacan's 'parle-être'), and subject *to* that order. But if there is division in the image, and instability in the pronoun, there is equally loss, and difficulty, in the word. Language can only operate by designating an object in its absence. Lacan takes this further, and states that symbolisation turns on the object *as* absence. He gives as his reference Freud's early account of the child's hallucinatory cathexis of the object for which it cries (Freud, I, 1895, p. 319), and his later description in *Beyond the Pleasure Principle* (Freud, XVIII, 1920, p. 14) of the child's symbolisation of the absent mother in play. In the first example, the child hallucinates the object it desires; in the second, it throws a cotton reel out of its cot in order to symbolise the absence and the presence of the mother. Symbolisation starts, therefore, when the child gets its first sense that something could be missing; words stand for objects, because they only have to be spoken at the moment when the first object is lost. For Lacan, the subject can only operate within language by constantly repeating that moment of fundamental and irreducible division. The subject is therefore constituted in language *as* this division or splitting (Freud's *Ichspaltung*, or splitting of the ego).

Lacan termed the order of language the symbolic, that of the ego and its identifications the imaginary (the stress, therefore, is quite deliberately on symbol and image, the idea of something which 'stands in'). The real was then his term for the moment of impossibility onto which both are grafted, the point of that moment's endless return.[2]

Lacan's account of childhood then follows his basic premise

2. This can be compared with, for example, Melanie Klein's account of symbol-formation (Klein, 1930), and also with Hannah Segal's (1957), where symbolisation is an effect of anxiety and a means of transcending it on the path to

that identity is constructed in language, but only at a cost. Identity shifts, and language speaks the loss which lay behind that first moment of symbolisation. When the child asks something of its mother, that loss will persist over and above anything which she can possibly give, or say, in reply. Demand always 'bears on something other than the satisfaction which it calls for' (MP, p. 80), and each time the demand of the child is answered by the satisfaction of its needs, so this 'something other' is relegated to the place of its original impossibility. Lacan terms this 'desire'. It can be defined as the 'remainder' of the subject, something which is always left over, but which has no content as such. Desire functions much as the zero unit in the numerical chain – its place is both constitutive *and* empty.

The concept of desire is crucial to Lacan's account of sexuality. He considered that the failure to grasp its implications leads inevitably to a reduction of sexuality back into the order of a need (something, therefore, which could be satisfied). Against this, he quoted Freud's statement: 'we must reckon with the possibility that something in the nature of the sexual instinct itself is unfavourable to the realisation of complete satisfaction' (Freud, XI, 1912, pp. 188–9; cit. PP p. 113).

At the same time 'identity' and 'wholeness' remain precisely at the level of fantasy. Subjects in language persist in their belief that somewhere there is a point of certainty, of knowledge and of truth. When the subject addresses its demand outside itself to another, this other becomes the fantasied place of just such a knowledge or certainty. Lacan calls this the Other – the site of language to which the speaking subject necessarily refers. The Other appears to hold the 'truth' of the subject and the power to make good its loss. But this is the ultimate fantasy. Language is the place where meaning circulates – the meaning of each lin-

---

reality, a path which is increasingly assured by the strengthening of the ego itself. Cf. also Lacan's specific critique of Ernest Jones's famous article on symbolism (Jones, 1916; *Ecrits* (1959)), which he criticised for its definition of language in terms of an increasing mastery or appropriation of reality, and for failing to see, therefore, the structure of metaphor (or substitution) which lies at the root of, and is endlessly repeated within, subjectivity in its relation to the unconscious. It is in this sense also that Lacan's emphasis on language should be differentiated from what he defined as 'culturalism', that is, from any conception of language as a social phenomenon which does not take into account its fundamental instability (language as constantly placing, and *displacing*, the subject).

guistic unit can only be established by reference to another, and it is arbitrarily fixed. Lacan, therefore, draws from Saussure's concept of the arbitrary nature of the linguistic sign (Saussure, 1915 (1974)), the implication that there can be no final guarantee or securing of language. There is, Lacan writes, 'no Other of the Other', and anyone who claims to take up this place is an imposter (the Master and/or psychotic).

Sexuality belongs in this area of instability played out in the register of demand and desire, each sex coming to stand, mythically and exclusively, for that which could satisfy and complete the other. It is when the categories 'male' and 'female' are seen to represent an absolute and complementary division that they fall prey to a mystification in which the difficulty of sexuality instantly disappears: 'to disguise this gap by relying on the virtue of the "genital" to resolve it through the maturation of tenderness . . . , however piously intended, is nonetheless a fraud' (MP, p. 81). Lacan therefore, argued that psychoanalysis should not try to produce 'male' and 'female' as complementary entities, sure of each other and of their own identity, but should expose the fantasy on which this notion rests.

As Juliet Mitchell describes above, there is a tendency, when arguing for the pre-given nature of sexual difference, for the specificity of male and female drives, to lose sight of the more radical aspects of Freud's work on sexuality – his insistence on the disjunction between the sexual object and the sexual aim, his difficult challenge to the concept of perversion, and his demand that heterosexual object-choice be explained and not assumed (Freud, VII, 1905, pp. 144–6, note 1, 1915). For Lacan, the 'vicissitudes' of the instinct ('instinct' was the original English translation for the German word 'trieb') cannot be understood as a deviation, accident or defence on the path to a normal heterosexuality which would ideally be secured. Rather the term 'vicissitude' indicates a fundamental difficulty inherent in human sexuality, which can be seen in the very concept of the drive.

The concept of the drive is crucial to the discussion of sexuality because of the relative ease with which it can be used to collapse psychoanalysis into biology, the dimension from which, for Lacan, it most urgently needed to be retrieved. He rejected the idea of a gradual 'maturation' of the drive, with its associated emphasis on genital identity (the 'virtue' of the genital) because of the way it implies a quasi-biological sequence of sexual life. Instead he stressed the resistance of the drive to any biological definition.

The drive is not the instinct precisely because it cannot be reduced to the order of need (Freud defined it as an internal stimulus only to distinguish it immediately from hunger and thirst). The drive is divisible into pressure, source, object and aim; and it challenges any straightforward concept of satisfaction – the drive can be sublimated and Freud described its object as 'indifferent'. What matters, therefore, is not what the drive *achieves*, but its *process*. For Lacan, that process reveals all the difficulty which characterises the subject's relationship to the Other. In his account, the drive is something in the nature of an appeal, or searching out, which always goes beyond the actual relationships on which it turns. Although Freud did at times describe the drive in terms of an economy of pleasure (the idea that tension is resolved when the drive achieves its aim), Lacan points to an opposite stress in Freud's work. In *Beyond the Pleasure Principle*, when Freud described the child's game with the cotton reel, what he identified in that game was a process of pure repetition which revolved around the object as lost. Freud termed this the death drive. Analysts since Freud (specifically Melanie Klein) have taken this to refer to a primordial instinct of aggression. For Freud there could be no such instinct, in that all instincts are characterised by their aggression, their tenacity or insistence (exactly their *drive*). It is this very insistence which places the drive outside any register of need, and beyond an economy of pleasure. The drive touches on an area of excess (it is 'too much'). Lacan calls this *jouissance* (literally 'orgasm', but used by Lacan to refer to something more than pleasure which can easily tip into its opposite).

In Lacan's description of the transformation of the drive (its stages), the emphasis is always on the loss of the object around which it revolves, and hence on the drive itself as a representation. Lacan therefore took one step further Freud's own assertion that the drive can only be understood in terms of the representation to which it is attached, by arguing that the structure of representation is present in the very process of the drive. For Lacan, there is always distance in the drive and always a reference to the Other (he added to the oral and anal drives the scopic and invocatory drives whose objects are the look and the voice). But because of its relation to the question of sexual difference, he made a special case for the genital drive in order to retrieve it from the residual biologism to which it is so easily assimilated: 'There is no genital drive. It can go and get f... [. . .] on the side of the Other' (SXI, p. 173, *p. 189*). In one of his final statements, Lacan again insisted that Freud had seen this, despite his equation of the genital and the reproductive at certain moments of his work (*Ornicar?*, 20–21, 1980, p. 16).[3]

When Lacan himself did refer to biology, it was in order to remind us of the paradox inherent in reproduction itself, which, as Freud pointed out, represents a victory of the species over the individual. The 'fact' of sexed reproduction marks the subject as '*subject to*' death (SXI, p. 186, *p. 205*). There is a parallel here with the subject's submission to language, just as there is an analogy between the endless circulation of the drive and the structure of meaning itself ('a topological unity of the gaps in play', SXI, p. 165, *p. 181*). At moments, therefore, it looks as if Lacan too is grounding his theory of representation in the biological facts of life. But the significant stress was away from this, to an understanding of how representation determines the limits within which we experience our sexual life. If there is no straightforward biological sequence, and no satisfaction of the drive, then the idea of a complete and assured sexual identity belongs in the realm of fantasy.

The structure of the drive and what Lacan calls the 'nodal point' of desire are the two concepts in his work as a whole which undermine a normative account of human sexuality, and they have repercussions right across the analytic setting. Lacan considered that an emphasis on genital maturation tends to produce a dualism of the analytic relationship which can only reinforce the imaginary identifications of the subject. It is clear from the first article translated here (IT) that the question of feminine sexuality brings with it that of psychoanalytic technique. Thus by insisting to Dora that she was in love with Herr K, Freud was not only defining her in terms of a normative concept of genital heterosexuality, he also failed to see his own place within the analytic relationship, and reduced it to a dual dimension operating on the axes of identification and demand. By asking Dora to realise her 'identity' through Herr K, Freud was simultaneously asking her

3. *Ornicar?*, periodical of the department of psychoanalysis, under Lacan's direction up to 1981, at the University of Paris VIII (Sorbonne) (Lacan, 1975–   ).

to meet, or reflect, his own demand. On both counts, he was binding her to a dual relationship in which the problem of desire has no place. For Lacan, there was always this risk that psychoanalysis will strengthen for the patient the idea of self completion through another, which was the fantasy behind the earliest mother–child relationship. If the analyst indicates to the patient that he or she 'desires this or that object' (SII, p. 267), this can only block the emergence of desire itself.

Lacan, therefore, defined the objective of analysis as the breaking of any imaginary relationship between patient and analyst through the intervention of a third term which throws them both onto the axis of the symbolic. The intervention of a third term is the precondition of language (the use of the three basic pronouns 'I'/'you'/'he-she-it'), and it can be seen in the structure of the Oedipus complex itself. What matters here, however, is that the symbolic sets a limit to the 'imaginary' of the analytic situation. Both analyst and patient must come to see how they are constituted by an order which goes beyond their interaction as such: 'The imaginary economy only has a meaning and we only have a relation to it in so far as it is inscribed in a symbolic order which imposes a ternary relation' (SII, p. 296).

By focusing on what he calls the symbolic order, Lacan was doing no more than taking to its logical conclusion Freud's preoccupation with an 'historic event' in the determination of human subjectivity, which Juliet Mitchell describes above. But for Lacan this is not some mythical moment of our past, it is the present order in which every individual subject must take up his or her place. His concern to break the duality of the analytic situation was part of his desire to bring this dimension back into the centre of our understanding of psychic life. The subject and the analytic process, must break out of the imaginary dyad which blinds them to what is happening outside. As was the case with Freud, the concept of castration came into Lacan's account of sexuality as the direct effect of this emphasis. For Lacan, the increasing stress on the mother–child relationship in analytic theory, and the rejection of the concept of castration had to be seen as related developments, because the latter only makes sense with reference to the wider symbolic order in which that relationship is played out:

Taking the experience of psychoanalysis in its development

over sixty years, it comes as no surprise to note that whereas the first outcome of its origins was a conception of the castration complex based on paternal repression, it has progressively directed its interests towards the frustrations coming from the mother, not that such a distortion has shed any light on the complex. (C, p. 87)

This was at the heart of Lacan's polemic. He considered that it was the failure to grasp the concept of the symbolic which has led psychoanalysis to concentrate increasingly on the adequacies and inadequacies of the mother-child relationship, an emphasis which tends to be complicit with the idea of a maternal role (the concept of mothering).[4] The concept of castration was central to Lacan because of the reference which it always contains to paternal law.

Addressing Melanie Klein, Lacan makes it clear that the argument for a reintroduction of the concept of desire into the definition of human sexuality is a return to, and a reformulation of, the law and the place of the father as it was originally defined by Freud ('a dimension . . . increasingly evaded since Freud', PP, p. 117):

Melanie Klein describes the relationship to the mother as a mirrored relationship: the maternal body becomes the receptacle of the drives which the child projects onto it, drives motivated by aggression born of a fundamental disappointment. This is to neglect the fact that the outside is given for the subject as the place where the desire of the Other is situated, and where he or she will encounter the third term, the father. (Lacan, 1957–8, p. 13)

4. Nancy Chodorow's reading of psychoanalysis for feminism (Chodorow, 1979) paradoxically also belongs here, and it touches on all the problems raised so far. The book attempts to use psychoanalysis to account for the acquisition and reproduction of mothering, but it can only do so by displacing the concepts of the unconscious and bisexuality in favour of a notion of gender imprinting ('the establishment of an unambiguous and unquestioned gender identity', p. 158 – the concept comes from Stoller (1965)), which is compatible with a sociological conception of role. Thus the problem needing to be addressed – the acquisition of sexual identity and its difficulty – is sidestepped in the account. The book sets itself to question sexual *roles*, but only within the limits of an assumed sexual *identity*.

Lacan argued, therefore, for a return to the concept of the father,
but this concept is now defined in relation to that of desire. What
matters is that the relationship of the child to the mother is not
simply based on 'frustration and satisfaction' ('the notion of
frustration (which was never employed by Freud)', MP, p. 80),
but on the recognition of her desire. The mother is refused to the
child in so far as a prohibition falls on the child's desire to be what
the mother desires (not the same, note, as a desire to possess or
enjoy the mother in the sense normally understood):

> What we meet as an accident in the child's development is
> linked to the fact that the child does not find himself or herself
> alone in front of the mother, and that the phallus forbids the
> child the satisfaction of his or her own desire, which is the
> desire to be the exclusive desire of the mother. (Lacan, 1957–8,
> p. 14)

The duality of the relation between mother and child
must be broken, just as the analytic relation must be thrown
onto the axis of desire. In Lacan's account, the phallus stands
for that moment of rupture. It refers mother and child to the
dimension of the symbolic which is figured by the father's
place. The mother is taken to desire the phallus not because she
contains it (Klein), but precisely because she does not. The
phallus therefore belongs somewhere else; it breaks the two
term relation and initiates the order of exchange. For Lacan,
it takes on this value as a function of the androcentric nature
of the symbolic order itself (cf. pp. 45–6 below). But its status
is in itself false, and must be recognised by the child as such.
Castration means first of all this – that the child's desire for the
mother does not refer *to* her but *beyond* her, to an object, the
phallus, whose status is first imaginary (the object presumed to
satisfy her desire) and then symbolic (recognition that desire
cannot be satisfied).

The place of the phallus in the account, therefore, follows from
Lacan's return to the position and law of the father, but this
concept has been reformulated in relation to that of desire. Lacan
uses the term 'paternal metaphor', metaphor having a very
specific meaning here. First, as a reference to the act of substitution (substitution is the very law of metaphoric operation),
whereby the prohibition of the father takes up the place

originally figured by the absence of the mother. Secondly, as a reference to the status of paternity itself which can only ever logically be *inferred*. And thirdly, as part of an insistence that the father stands for a place and a function which is not reducible to the presence or absence of the real father as such:

> To speak of the Name of the Father is by no means the same thing as invoking paternal deficiency (which is often done). We know today that an Oedipus complex can be constituted perfectly well even if the father is not there, while originally it was the excessive presence of the father which was held responsible for all dramas. But it is not in an environmental perspective that the answer to these questions can be found. So as to make the link between the Name of the Father, in so far as he can at times be missing, and the father whose effective presence is not always necessary for him not to be missing, I will introduce the expression *paternal metaphor*. (Lacan, 1957–8, p. 8)

Finally, the concept is used to separate the father's function from the idealised or imaginary father with which it is so easily confused and which is exactly the figure to be got round, or past: 'Any discourse on the Oedipus complex which fails to bring out this figure will be inscribed within the very effects of the complex' (Safouan, 1974, p. 9).

Thus when Lacan calls for a return to the place of the father he is crucially distinguishing himself from any sociological conception of role. The father is a function and refers to a law, the place outside the imaginary dyad and against which it breaks. To make of him a referent is to fall into an ideological trap: the 'prejudice which falsifies the conception of the Oedipus complex from the start, by making it define as natural, rather than normative, the predominance of the paternal figure' (IT, p. 69).

There is, therefore, no assumption about the ways in which the places come to be fulfilled (it is this very assumption which is questioned). This is why, in talking of the genetic link between the mother and child, Lacan could refer to the 'vast social connivance' which *makes* of her the 'privileged site of prohibitions' (SXVIII, 6, p. 10).[5] And why Safouan, in an article on the

5. References to Lacan's Seminars XVIII ('L'envers de la psychanalyse', Lacan, 1969–70) and XXI ('Les non-dupes errent', Lacan, 1973–4) (unpublished typescripts) are given to the week, and the page, of the typescript.

function of the real father, recognises that it is the intervention of the third term which counts, and that nothing of itself requires that this should be embodied by the father as such (Safouan, 1974, p. 127). Lacan's positon should be read against two alternative emphases – on the actual behaviour of the mother alone (adequacy and inadequacy), and on a literally present or absent father (his idealisation and/or deficiency).

The concept of the phallus and the castration complex can only be understood in terms of this reference to prohibition and the law, just as rejection of these concepts tends to lose sight of this reference. The phallus needs to be placed on the axis of desire before it can be understood, or questioned, as the differential mark of sexual identification (boy or girl, having or not having the phallus). By breaking the imaginary dyad, the phallus represents a moment of division (Lacan calls this the subject's 'lack-in-being') which re-enacts the fundamental splitting of subjectivity itself. And by jarring against any naturalist account of sexuality ('phallocentrism . . . strictly impossible to deduce from any pre-established harmony of the said psyche to the nature it expresses', *Ecrits* (1955–6), pp. 554–5, *p. 198*), the phallus relegates sexuality to a strictly other dimension – the order of the symbolic outside of which, for Lacan, sexuality cannot be understood. The importance of the phallus is that its status in the development of human sexuality is something which nature *cannot* account for.

When Lacan is reproached with phallocentrism at the level of his theory, what is most often missed is that the subject's entry into the symbolic order is equally an exposure of the value of the phallus itself. The subject has to recognise that there is desire, or lack in the place of the Other, that there is no ultimate certainty or truth, and that the status of the phallus is a fraud (this is, for Lacan, the meaning of castration). The phallus can only take up its place by indicating the precariousness of any identity assumed by the subject on the basis of its token. Thus the phallus stands for that moment when prohibition must function, in the sense of whom may be assigned to whom in the triangle made up of mother, father and child, but at that same moment it signals to the subject that 'having' only functions at the price of a loss and 'being' as an effect of division. Only if this is dropped from the account can the phallus be taken to represent an unproblematic assertion of male privilege, or else lead to reformulations intended to guarantee the continuity of sexual development for both sexes (Jones).

It is that very continuity which is challenged in the account given here. The concept of the phallus and the castration complex testify above all to the problematic nature of the subject's insertion into his or her sexual identity, to an impossibility writ large over that insertion at the point where it might be taken to coincide with the genital drive. Looking back at Jones's answer to Freud, it is clear that his opposition to Freud's concept of the phallic phase involves a rejection of the dimension of desire, of the loss of the object, of the difficulty inherent in subjectivity itself (the argument of the first article from *Scilicet* translated here (PP)).[6] Just as it was Freud's failure to apply the concept of castration literally to the girl child which brought him up against the concept of desire (the argument of the second article (FS)).

The subject then takes up his or her identity with reference to the phallus, but that identity is thereby designated symbolic (it is something enjoined on the subject). Lacan inverts Saussure's formula for the linguistic sign (the opposition between signifier and signified), giving primacy to the signifier over that which it signifies (or rather creates in that act of signification). For it is essential to his argument that sexual difference is a legislative divide which creates and reproduces its categories. Thus Lacan replaces Saussure's model for the arbitrary nature of the linguistic sign:

TREE

(which is indeed open to the objection that it seems to reflect a theory of language based on a correspondence between words and things), with this model (*Ecrits* (1957), p. 499, *p. 151*):

6. *Scilicet*, review of Lacan's series, *le champ freudien* (Lacan, 1968–76).

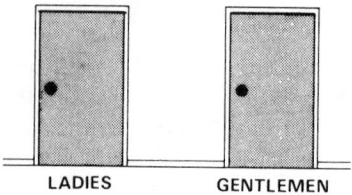

LADIES   GENTLEMEN

'Any speaking being whatever' (*E*, p. 150) must line up on one or other side of the divide.[7]

Sexual difference is then assigned according to whether individual subjects do or do not possess the phallus, which means not that anatomical difference *is* sexual difference (the one as strictly deducible from the other), but that anatomical difference comes to *figure* sexual difference, that is, it becomes the sole representative of what that difference is allowed to be. It thus covers over the complexity of the child's early sexual life with a crude opposition in which that very complexity is refused or repressed. The phallus thus indicates the reduction of difference to an instance of visible perception, a *seeming* value.

Freud gave the moment when boy and girl child saw that they were different the status of a trauma in which the girl is seen to be lacking (the objections often start here). But something can only be *seen* to be missing according to a pre-existing hierarchy of values ('there is nothing missing in the real', PP, p. 113). What counts is not the perception but its already assigned meaning – the moment therefore belongs in the symbolic. And if Lacan states that the symbolic usage of the phallus stems from its visibility (something for which he was often criticised), it is only in so far as the order of the visible, the apparent, the seeming is the object of his attack. In fact he constantly refused any crude identification of the phallus with the order of the visible or real ('one might say that this signifier is chosen as what stands out as most easily seized upon in the real of sexual copulation', MP, p. 82), and he referred it instead to that function of 'veiling' in which he locates the fundamental duplicity of the linguistic sign:

7. It is not, therefore, a question of philology and *then* the phallus, as John Forrester argues, but of sexuality/the phallus *as* language (John Forrester, 'Philology and the phallus', in MacCabe (1981)).

All these propositions merely veil over the fact that the phallus can only play its role as veiled, that is, as in itself the sign of the latency with which everything signifiable is struck as soon as it is raised to the function of signifier. (MP, p. 82)

Meaning is only ever erected, it is set up and fixed. The phallus symbolises the effects of the signifier in that having no value in itself, it can represent that to which value *accrues*.

Lacan's statements on language need to be taken in two directions – towards the fixing of meaning itself (that which is enjoined on the subject), and away from that very fixing to the point of its constant slippage, the risk or vanishing-point which it always contains (the unconscious). Sexuality is placed on both these dimensions at once. The difficulty is to hold these two emphases together – sexuality in the symbolic (an ordering), sexuality as that which constantly fails. Once the relationship between these two aspects of psychoanalysis can be seen, then the terms in which feminine sexuality can be described undergo a radical shift. The concept of the symbolic states that the woman's sexuality is inseparable from the representations through which it is produced ('images and symbols *for* the woman cannot be isolated from images and symbols *of* the woman . . . it is the representation of sexuality which conditions how it comes into play', C, p. 90), but those very representations will reveal the splitting through which they are constituted as such. The question of what a woman is in this account always stalls on the crucial acknowledgement that there is absolutely no guarantee that she *is* at all (cf. below pp. 48–50). But if she takes up her place according to the process described, then her sexuality will betray, necessarily, the impasses of its history.

Sexuality belongs for Lacan in the realm of masquerade. The term comes from Joan Rivière (Rivière, 1929) for whom it indicated a failed femininity. For Lacan, masquerade is the very definition of 'femininity' precisely because it is constructed with reference to a male sign. The question of frigidity (on which, Lacan recognised, psychoanalysis 'gave up', C, p. 89) also belongs here, and it is described in 'The Meaning of the Phallus' (MP) as the effect of the status of the phallic term. But this does not imply that there is a physiology to which women could somehow be returned, or into which they could be freed. Rather the term 'frigidity' stands, on the side of the woman, for the difficulty inherent in sexuality itself, the disjunction laid over the body by desire, at the point where it is inscribed into the genital relation. Psychoanalysis now recognises that any simple criterion of femininity in terms of a shift of pleasure from clitoris to vagina is a travesty, but what matters is the fantasies implicated in either (or both). For both sexes, sexuality will necessarily touch on the duplicity which underpins its fundamental divide. As for 'normal' vaginal femininity, which might be taken as the recognition of the value of the male sign (a 'coming to' that recognition), it will always evoke the splitting on which its value is erected ('why not acknowledge that if there is no virility which castration does not consecrate, then for the woman it is a castrated lover or a dead man . . . who hides behind the veil where he calls on her adoration', C, p. 95).

The description of feminine sexuality is, therefore, an exposure of the terms of its definition, the very opposite of a demand as to what that sexuality should be. Where such a definition is given – 'identification with her mother as desiring and a recognition of the phallus in the real father' (Safouan, 1976, p. 110), it involves precisely a collapse of the phallus into the real and of desire into recognition – giving the lie, we could say, to the whole problem outlined.[8]

II

Three points emerge from what has been described so far:

1. anatomy is what figures in the account: 'for me "anatomy is not destiny", but that does not mean that anatomy does not figure' (Safouan, 1976, p. 131), but it _only figures_ (it is a sham);
2. the phallus stands at its own expense and any male privilege erected upon it is an imposture 'what might be called a man, the male speaking being, strictly disappears as an effect of discourse, . . . by being inscribed within it solely as castration' (SXVIII, 12, p. 4);
3. woman is not inferior, she is _subjected_:

---

8. The difficulty of these terms is recognised by Safouan, but the problem remains; cf. also Eugénie Lemoine-Luccioni, _Partage des femmes_ (1976), where there is the same collapse between the Other to be recognised by the woman in her advent to desire, and the real man whom, ideally, she comes to accept

That the woman should be inscribed in an order of exchange of which she is the object, is what makes for the fundamentally conflictual, and, I would say, insoluble, character of her position: the symbolic order literally submits her, it transcends her . . . . There is for her something insurmountable, something unacceptable, in the fact of being placed as an object in a symbolic order to which, at the same time, she is subjected just as much as the man. (SII, pp. 304–5)

It is the strength of the concept of the symbolic that it systematically repudiates any account of sexuality which assumes the pre-given nature of sexual difference – the polemic within psychoanalysis and the challenge to any such 'nature' by feminism appear at their closest here. But a problem remains. Lacan's use of the symbolic at this stage relied heavily on Lévi-Strauss's notion of kinship in which women are defined as objects of exchange. As such it is open to the same objections as Lévi-Strauss's account in that it presupposes the subordination which it is intended to explain.[9] Thus while at first glance these remarks by Lacan seem most critical of the order described, they are in another sense complicit with that order and any argument constructed on their basis is likely to be circular.[10]

I think it is crucial that at the point where Lacan made these remarks he had a concept of full speech, of access to the symbolic order whose subjective equivalent is a successful linguistic

('the Other, the man', p. 83; 'the Other, the man as subject', p. 87). There seems to be a constant tendency to literalise the terms of Lacan's account and it is when this happens that the definitions most easily recognised as reactionary tend to appear. We can see this in such apparently different areas as Maude Mannoni's translation of the Name of the Father into a therapeutic practice which seeks to establish the paternal genealogy of the psychotic child (Mannoni, 1967), and in Lemoine-Luccioni's account of the real Other who ensures castration to the woman otherwise condemned to pure narcissism. Lemoine-Luccioni's account is in many ways reminiscent of that of Helene Deutsch (1930) who described the transition to femininity in terms of a desire for castration which is produced across the woman's body by the man.

9. See Elizabeth Cowie, 'Woman as Sign' (1978).
10. Cf. for example, Gayle Rubin, 'The Traffic in Women' in R. M. Reiter (1975), which describes psychoanalysis as a 'theory about the reproduction of kinship', losing sight, again, of the concept of the unconscious and the whole problem of sexual identity, reducing the relations described to a quite literal set of acts of exchange.

exchange (*Ecrits*, (1953)). But his work underwent a shift, which totally undercut any such conception of language as mediation, in favour of an increasing stress on its fundamental division, and the effects of that division on the level of sexuality itself.

'There is no sexual relation' – this became the emphasis of his account. 'There is no sexual relation' because the unconscious divides subjects to and from each other, and because it is the myth of that relation which acts as a barrier against the division, setting up a unity through which this division is persistently disavowed. Hence the related and opposite formula 'There is something of One' (the two formulas should be taken together) which refers to that fantasied unity of relation '*We are as one*. Of course everyone knows that it has never happened for two to make one, but still *we are as one*. That's what the idea of love starts out from . . . the problem then being how on earth there could be love for another', (SXX, p. 46), to its suppression of division and difference ('Love your neighbour as yourself . . . the commandment lays down the abolition of sexual difference', SXXI, 4, p. 3), to the very ideology of oneness and completion which, for Lacan, closes off the gap of human desire.

In the earlier texts, the unity was assigned to the imaginary, the symbolic was at least potentially its break. In the later texts, Lacan located the fantasy of 'sameness' within language and the sexual relation at one and the same time. 'There is no sexual relation' because subjects relate through what makes sense in *lalangue*.[11] This 'making sense' is a supplement, a making good of the lack of subjectivity and language, of the subject *in* language, against which lack it is set. Psychoanalysis states meaning to be sexual but it has left behind any notion of a repressed sexuality which it would somehow allow to speak. Meaning can only be described as sexual by taking the limits of meaning into account, for meaning in itself operates *at* the limit, the limits of its own failing: 'Meaning indicates the direction in which it fails', *E*, p. 150. The stress, therefore, is on the constant failing within

11. Lacan's term for Saussure's *langue* (language) from the latter's distinction between *langue* (the formal organisation of language) and *parole* (speech), the individual utterance. Lacan's term displaces this opposition in so far as, for him, the organisation of language can only be understood in terms of the subject's relationship to it. *Lalangue* indicates that part of language which reflects the laws of unconscious processes, but whose effects go beyond that reflection, and escape the grasp of the subject (see SXX, pp. 126–7).

language and sexuality, which meaning attempts to supplement or conceal: 'Everything implied by the analytic engagement with human behaviour indicates not that meaning reflects the sexual but that it makes up for it' (SXXI, 15, p. 9). Sexuality is the vanishing-point of meaning. Love, on the other hand, belongs to the *Lust-Ich* or pleasure-ego which disguises that failing in the reflection of like to like (love as the ultimate form of self-recognition).

We could say that Lacan has taken the relationship between the unconscious and sexuality and has pushed it to its furthest extreme, producing an account of sexuality solely in terms of its divisions – the division *of* the subject, division *between* subjects (as opposed to relation). Hence the increasing focus on enunciation,[12] on language's internal division (see the graph on p. 132), and also the deliberate formalisation of the account – sexual difference as a divide, something to be laid out (exactly a formality, a question of form (the graph of *Encore*, SXX, *E*, p. 149)). The challenge to the unity of the subject, its seeming coherence, is then addressed to the discourse of sexuality itself: 'instead of one signifier we need to interrogate, we should interrogate the signifier *One*' (SXX, p. 23). Thus there is no longer imaginary 'unity' and then symbolic difference or exchange, but rather an indictment of the symbolic for the imaginary unity which its most persistent myths continue to promote.

Within this process, woman is constructed as an absolute category (excluded and elevated at one and the same time), a category which serves to guarantee that unity on the side of the man. The man places the woman at the basis of his fantasy, or constitutes fantasy through the woman. Lacan moved away, therefore, from the idea of a problematic but socially assured process of exchange (women as objects) to the construction of woman as a category within language (woman as *the* object, the fantasy of her definition). What is now exposed in the account is 'a carrying over onto the woman of the difficulty inherent in sexuality' itself (PP, p. 118).

12. The term comes from Benveniste (Benveniste, 1958), his distinction between *énoncé* and *énonciation*, between the subject of the statement and the subject of the utterance itself. Lacan sites the unconscious at the radical division of these instances, seen at its most transparent in the statement 'I am lying' where there are clearly two subjects, one who is lying and one who is not.

The last two texts translated here (*E* and *O*) belong to this development. They go further than, and can be seen as an attempt to take up the problems raised by, those that precede them. For whereas in the earlier texts the emphasis was on the circulation of the phallus in the process of sexual exchange, in these texts it is effectively stated that if it is the phallus that circulates then there is no exchange (or relation). The question then becomes not so much the 'difficulty' of feminine sexuality consequent on phallic division, as what it means, given that division, to speak of the 'woman' at all. It is, as the author of the first article from *Scilicet* hints at the end of the argument, in many ways a more fundamental or 'radical' enquiry:

> whatever can be stated about the constitution of the feminine position in the Oedipus complex or in the sexual 'relation' concerns only a second stage, one in which the rules governing a certain type of exchange based on a common value have already been established. It is at a more radical stage, constitutive of those very rules themselves, that Freud points to one last question by indicating that it is the woman who comes to act as their support. (PP, p. 118–19)

In the later texts, the central term is the *object small a [objet a]*, Lacan's formula for the lost object which underpins symbolisation, cause of and 'stand in' for desire. What the man relates to is this object and the 'whole of his realisation in the sexual relation comes down to fantasy' (*E*, p. 157). As the place onto which lack is projected, and through which it is simultaneously disavowed, woman is a 'symptom' for the man.

Defined as such, reduced to being nothing other than this fantasmatic place, the woman does not exist. Lacan's statement 'The woman does not exist' is, therefore, the corollary of his accusation, or charge, against sexual fantasy. It means, not that women do not exist, but that her status as an absolute category and guarantor of fantasy (exactly *The* woman) is false (The). Lacan sees courtly love as the elevation of the woman into the place where her absence or inaccessibility stands in for male lack ('For the man, whose lady was entirely, in the most servile sense of the term, his female subject, courtly love is the only way of coming off elegantly from the absence of sexual relation', *E*, p. 141), just as he sees her denigration as the precondition for man's belief in his own soul ('For the soul to come into being, she, the woman, is differentiated from it . . . called woman and defamed', *E*, p. 156). In relation to the man, woman comes to stand for both difference and loss: 'On the one hand, the woman becomes, or is produced, precisely as what he is not, that is, sexual difference, and on the other, as what he has to renounce, that is, *jouissance*' (SXVIII, 6, pp. 9–10).[13]

Within the phallic definition, the woman is constituted as 'not all', in so far as the phallic function rests on an exception (the 'not') which is assigned to her. Woman is excluded *by* the nature of words, meaning that the definition poses her as exclusion. Note that this is not the same thing as saying that woman is excluded *from* the nature of words, a misreading which leads to the recasting of the whole problem in terms of woman's place outside language, the idea that women might have of themselves an entirely different speech.

For Lacan, men and women are only ever in language ('Men and women are signifiers bound to the common usage of language', SXX, p. 36). All speaking beings must line themselves up on one side or the other of this division, but anyone can cross over and inscribe themselves on the opposite side from that to which they are anatomically destined.[14] It is, we could say, an either/or situation, but one whose fantasmatic nature was endlessly reiterated by Lacan: 'these are not positions able to satisfy us, so much so that we can state the unconscious to be defined by the fact that it has a much clearer idea of what is going on than the truth that man is not woman' (SXXI, 6, p. 9).

The woman, therefore, is *not*, because she is defined purely against the man (she is the negative of that definition – 'man is *not* woman'), and because this very definition is designated fantasy, a set which may well be empty (the reference to set theory in the seminar from *Ornicar?* translated here (O)). If woman is 'not all',

13. See Otto Fenichel, in a paper to which Lacan often referred, on the refusal of difference which underpins the girl = phallus equation frequently located as a male fantasy: 'the differentness of women is denied in both cases; in the one case, in the attempt to repress women altogether, in the other, in denying their individuality' (Fenichel, 1949, p. 13).
14. Note how this simultaneously shifts the concept of bisexuality – not an undifferentiated sexual nature prior to symbolic difference (Freud's earlier sense), but the availability to all subjects of both positions in relation to that difference itself.

writes Lacan, then 'she' can hardly refer to all women.

As negative to the man, woman becomes a total object of fantasy (or an object of total fantasy), elevated into the place of the Other and made to stand for its truth. Since the place of the Other is also the place of God, this is the ultimate form of mystification ('the more man may ascribe to the woman in confusion with God . . . the less he is', *E*, p. 160). In so far as God 'has not made his exit' (*E*, p. 154), so the woman becomes the support of his symbolic place. In his later work Lacan defined the objective of psychoanalysis as breaking the confusion behind this mystification, a rupture between the *object a* and the Other, whose conflation he saw as the elevation of fantasy into the order of truth. The *object a*, cause of desire and support of male fantasy gets transposed onto the image of the woman as Other who then acts as its guarantee. The absolute 'Otherness' of the woman, therefore, serves to secure for the man his own self-knowledge and truth. Remember that for Lacan there can be no such guarantee – there is no 'Other of the Other' (cf. p. 33 above). His rejection of the category 'Woman', therefore, belonged to his assault on any unqualified belief in the Other as such: 'This ~~The~~ [of the woman] crossed through . . . relates to the signifier O when it is crossed through $(\emptyset)$' (*E*, p. 151).

Increasingly this led Lacan to challenge the notions of 'knowledge' and 'belief', and the myths on which they necessarily rely. All Lacan's statements in the last two translated texts against belief in the woman, against her status as knowing, problematic as they are, can only be understood as part of this constant undercutting of the terms on which they rest. In these later texts, Lacan continually returns to the 'subject supposed to know', the claim of a subject to know (the claim to know oneself as subject), and the different forms of discourse which can be organised around this position (see note 6. p. 161).[15] 'Knowing' is only

---

15. Much of the difficulty of Lacan's work stemmed from his attempt to subvert that position from within his own utterance, to rejoin the place of 'non-knowledge' which he designated the unconscious, by the constant slippage or escape of his speech, and thereby to undercut the very mastery which his own position as speaker (master and analyst) necessarily constructs. In fact one can carry out the same operation on the statement 'I do not know' as Lacan performed on the utterance 'I am lying' (cf. note 12, p. 47 above) – for, if I do not know, then how come I know enough to know that I do not know and if I do know that I do not know, then it is not true that I do not know. Lacan was undoubtedly trapped in this paradox of his own utterance.

ever such a claim, just as 'belief' rests entirely on the supposition of what is false. To believe in The Woman is simply a way of closing off the division or uncertainty which also underpins conviction as such. And when Lacan says that women do not know, while, at one level, he relegates women outside, and against, the very mastery of his own statement, he was also recognising the binding, or restricting, of the parameters of knowledge itself ('masculine knowledge irredeemably an erring', SXXI, 6, p. 11).

The Other crossed through ($\emptyset$) stands against this knowledge as the place of division where meaning falters, where it slips and shifts. It is the place of *signifiance*, Lacan's term for this very movement in language against, or away from, the positions of coherence which language simultaneously constructs. The Other therefore stands against the phallus – its pretence to meaning and false consistency. It is from the Other that the phallus seeks authority and is refused.

The woman belongs on the side of the Other in this second sense, for in so far as *jouissance* is defined as phallic so she might be said to belong somewhere else. The woman is implicated, of necessity, in phallic sexuality, but at the same time it is 'elsewhere that she upholds the question of her own *jouissance*' (PP, p. 121), that is, the question of her status as desiring subject. Lacan designates this *jouissance* supplementary so as to avoid any notion of complement, of woman as a complement to man's phallic nature (which is precisely the fantasy). But it is also a recognition of the 'something more', the 'more than *jouisssance*',[16] which Lacan locates in the Freudian concept of repetition – what escapes or is left over from the phallic function, and exceeds it. Woman is, therefore, placed *beyond* (beyond the phallus). That 'beyond' refers at once to her most total mystification as absolute Other (and hence nothing other than other), and to a *question*, the question of her own *jouissance*, of her greater or lesser access to the residue of the dialectic to which she is constantly subjected. The problem is that once the notion of 'woman' has been so relentlessly exposed as a fantasy, then any such question becomes an almost impossible one to pose.

Lacan's reference to woman as Other needs, therefore, to be

16. At times *jouissance* is opposed to the idea of pleasure as the site of this excess, but where *jouissance* is defined as phallic, Lacan introduces the concept of the supplement ('more than') with which to oppose it.

seen as an attempt to hold apart two moments which are in
constant danger of collapsing into each other – that which assigns
woman to the negative place of its own (phallic) system, and that
which asks the question as to whether women might, as a very
effect of that assignation, break against and beyond that system
itself. For Lacan, that break is always within language, it is the
break of the subject *in* language. The concept of *jouissance* (what
escapes in sexuality) and the concept of *signifiance* (what shifts
within language) are inseparable.

Only when this is seen can we properly locate the tension
which runs right through the chapters translated here from
Lacan's Seminar XX, *Encore* (*E*), between his critique of the
forms of mystification latent to the category Woman, and the
repeated question as to what her 'otherness' might be. A tension
which can be recognised in the very query 'What does a woman
want?' on which Freud stalled and to which Lacan returned. That
tension is clearest in Lacan's appeal to St Theresa, whose statue
by Bernini in Rome[17] he took as the model for an-other *jouissance*
– the woman therefore as 'mystical' but, he insisted, this is not
'not political' (*E*, p. 146), in so far as mysticism is one of the
available forms of expression where such 'otherness' in sexuality
utters its most forceful complaint. And if we cut across for a
moment from Lacan's appeal to her image as executed by the
man, to St Theresa's own writings, to her commentary on 'The
Song of Songs', we find its sexuality in the form of a disturbance
which, crucially, she locates not on the level of the sexual content
of the song, but on the level of its enunciation, in the instability of
its pronouns – a precariousness in language which reveals that
neither the subject nor God can be placed ('speaking with one
person, asking for peace from another, and then speaking to the
person in whose presence she is' (Saint Theresa, 1946, p. 359)).[18]
Sexuality belongs, therefore, on the level of its, and the subject's ,
shifting.

17. 'What is her *jouissance*, her *coming* from?' (*E*, p. 147) – a question made
    apparently redundant by the angel with arrow poised above her (the
    'piercing' of Saint Theresa), and one whose problematic nature is best
    illustrated by the cardinals and doges, in the gallery on either side of the
    'proscenium' – *witnesses* to the staging of an act which, because of the
    perspective lines, they cannot actually *see* (Bernini, 'The Ecstasy of Saint
    Theresa', Santa Maria della Vittoria, Rome).
18. Commentary on the line from the 'Song of Songs' – 'Let the Lord kiss me
    with the kiss of his mouth, for thy breasts are sweeter than wine'.

Towards the end of his work, Lacan talked of woman's 'anti-phallic' nature, as leaving her open to that 'which of the unconscious cannot be spoken' (*Ornicar?*, 20–1, p. 12) (a reference to women analysts in which we can recognise, ironically, the echo of Freud's conviction that they would have access to a different strata of psychic life).[19] In relation to the earlier texts we could say that woman no longer masquerades, she *defaults*: 'the *jouissance* of the woman does not go without saying, that is, without the saying of truth', whereas for the man 'his *jouissance* suffices which is precisely why he understands nothing' (SXXI, 7, p. 16). There is a risk, here, of giving back to the woman a status as truth (the very mythology denounced). But for Lacan, this 'truth' of the unconscious is only ever that moment of fundamental division through which the subject entered into language and sexuality, and the constant failing of position within both.

This is the force of Lacan's account – his insistence that femininity can only be understood in terms of its construction, an insistence which produced in reply the same reinstatement of women, the same argument for *her* sexual nature as was seen in the 1920s and 1930s in response to Freud. This time the question of symbolisation, which, we have argued, was latent to the earlier debate, has been at the centre of that response. This is all the more clear in that the specificity of feminine sexuality in the more recent discussion[20] has explicitly become the issue of women's relationship to language. In so far as it is the order of

19. At the time of writing Lacan had just dissolved his school in Paris, rejoining in the utterance through which he represented that act – 'Je père-sévère' ('I persevere' – the pun is on 'per' and 'père' (father)) – the whole problem of mastery and paternity which has cut across the institutional history of his work. From the early stand against a context which he (and others) considered authoritarian, and the cancellation, as its effect, of his seminar on the Name of the Father in 1953, to the question of mastery and transference which lay behind the further break in 1964, and which so clearly surfaces in the dissolution here. It has been the endless paradox of Lacan's position that he has provided the most systematic critique of forms of identification and transference which, by dint of this very fact, he has come most totally to represent. That a number of women analysts (cf. note 20 p. 54) have found their position in relation to this to be an impossible one, only confirms the close relation between the question of feminine sexuality and the institutional divisions and difficulties of psychoanalysis itself.

20. In this last section I will be referring predominately to the work of Michèle Montrelay and Luce Irigaray, the former a member of Lacan's school prior to its dissolution in January 1980 when she dissociated herself from him, the

language which structures sexuality around the male term, or the privileging of that term which shows sexuality to be constructed within language, so this raises the issue of women's relationship to that language and that sexuality simultaneously. The question of the body of the girl child (what she may or may not know of that body) as posed in the earlier debate, becomes the question of the woman's body as language (what, of that body, can achieve symbolisation). The objective is to retrieve the woman from the dominance of the phallic term and from language at one and the same time. What this means is that femininity is assigned to a point of origin prior to the mark of symbolic difference and the law. The privileged relationship of women to that origin gives them access to an archaic form of expressivity outside the circuit of linguistic exchange.

This point of origin is the maternal body, an undifferentiated space, and yet one in which the girl child recognises herself. The girl then has to suppress or devalue that fullness of recognition in order to line up within the order of the phallic term. In the argument for a primordial femininity, it is clear that the relation between the mother and child is conceived of as dyadic and simply reflective (one to one – the girl child fully *knows* herself in the mother) which once again precludes the concept of desire. Feminine specificity is, therefore, predicated directly onto the concept of an unmediated and unproblematic relation to origin.

The positions taken up have not been identical, but they have a shared stress on the specificity of the feminine drives, a stress which was at the basis of the earlier response to Freud. They take a number of their concepts directly from that debate (the concept of concentric feminine drives in Montrelay comes directly from Jones and Klein). But the effects of the position are different. Thus whereas for Jones, for example, those drives ideally

latter working within his school up to 1974 when she was dismissed from the newly reorganised department of psychoanalysis at the University of Paris VIII (Vincennes) on publication of her book, *Speculum de l'autre femme* (1974). Both are practising psychoanalysts. Montrelay takes up the Freud–Jones controversy specifically in terms of women's access to language in her article 'Inquiry into Femininity' (1970 (1978)). Irigaray's book *Speculum* contained a critique of Freud's papers on femininity; her later *Ce sexe qui n'en est pas un* (1977) contains a chapter ('Cosi fan tutti') directly addressed to Lacan's SXX, *Encore*.

anticipated and ensured the heterosexual identity of the girl child, now those same drives put at risk her access to any object at all (Montrelay)[21] or else they secure the woman to herself and, through that, to other women (Irigaray). Women are *returned*, therefore, in the account and to each other – against the phallic term but also against the loss of origin which Lacan's account is seen to imply. It is therefore a refusal of division which gives the woman access to a different strata of language, where words and things are not differentiated, and the real of the maternal body threatens or holds off woman's access to prohibition and the law.

There is a strength in this account, which has been recognised by feminism. At its most forceful it expresses a protest engendered by the very cogency of what Freud and then Lacan describe (it is the *effect* of that description).[22] And something of its position was certainly present in Lacan's earlier texts ('feminine sexuality . . . as the effort of a *jouissance* wrapped in its own contiguity', C, p. 97). But Lacan came back to this response in the later texts, which can therefore be seen as a sort of reply, much as Freud's 1931 and 1933 papers on femininity addressed some of the criticisms which he had received.

For Lacan, as we have seen, there is no pre-discursive reality ('How return, other than by means of a special discourse, to a pre-discursive reality?', SXX, p. 33), no place prior to the law which is available and can be retrieved. And there is no feminine outside language. First, because the unconscious severs the subject from any unmediated relation to the body as such ('there is nothing in the unconscious which accords with the body', O, p. 165), and secondly because the 'feminine' is constituted as a division in language, a division which produces the feminine as its negative term. If woman is defined as other it is because the

21. Montrelay attempts to resolve the 'Freud–Jones' controversy by making the two different accounts of femininity equal to *stages* in the girl's psychosexual development, femininity being defined as the passage from a concentric psychic economy to one in which symbolic castration has come into play. Access to symbolisation depends on the transition, and it is where it fails that the woman remains bound to a primordial cathexis of language as the extension of the undifferentiated maternal body. Montrelay should, therefore, be crucially distinguished from Irigaray at this point, since for her such a failure is precipitant of anxiety and is in no sense a concept of femininity which she is intending to promote.

22. Note too the easy slippage from Irigaray's title *Ce sexe qui n'en est pas un*, 'This sex which isn't one', to Lacan's formula, 'This sex which isn't *one*'.

definition produces her as other, and not because she has another essence. Lacan does not refuse difference ('if there was no difference how could I say there was no sexual relation', SXXI, 4, p. 18), but for him what is to be questioned is the seeming 'consistency' of that difference – of the body or anything else – the division it enjoins, the definitions of the woman it produces.

For Lacan, to say that difference is 'phallic' difference is to expose the symbolic and arbitrary nature of its division as such. It is crucial – and it is something which can be seen even more clearly in the response to the texts translated here – that refusal of the phallic term brings with it an attempt to reconstitute a form of subjectivity free of division, and hence a refusal of the notion of symbolisation itself. If the status of the phallus is to be challenged, it cannot, therefore, be directly from the feminine body but must be by means of a different symbolic term (in which case the relation to the body is immediately thrown into crisis), or else by an entirely different logic altogether (in which case one is no longer in the order of symbolisation at all).

The demands against Lacan therefore collapse two different levels of objection – that the body should be mediated by language and that the privileged term of that mediation be male. The fact that refusal of the phallus turns out once again to be a refusal of the symbolic does not close, but leaves open as still unanswered, the question as to why that necessary symbolisation and the privileged status of the phallus appear as interdependent in the structuring and securing (never secure) of human subjectivity.

There is, therefore, no question of denying here that Lacan was implicated in the phallocentrism he described, just as his own utterance constantly rejoins the mastery which he sought to undermine. The question of the unconscious and of sexuality, the movement towards and against them, operated at exactly this level of his own speech. But for Lacan they function as the question of that speech, and cannot be referred back to a body outside language, a place to which the 'feminine', and through that, women, might escape. In the response to Lacan, therefore, the 'feminine' has returned as it did in the 1920s and 1930s in reply to Freud, but this time with the added meaning of a resistance to a phallic organisation of sexuality which is recognised as such. The 'feminine' stands for a refusal of that organisation, its ordering, its identity. For Lacan, on the other hand, interrogating that same organisation undermines any absolute definition of the 'feminine' at all.

Psychoanalysis does not produce that definition. It gives an account of how that definition is produced. While the objection to its dominant term must be recognised, it cannot be answered by an account which returns to a concept of the feminine as pre-given, nor by a mandatory appeal to an androcentrism in the symbolic which the phallus would simply reflect. The former relegates women outside language and history, the latter simply subordinates them to both.

In these texts Lacan gives an account of how the status of the phallus in human sexuality enjoins on the woman a definition in which she is simultaneously symptom and myth. As long as we continue to feel the effects of that definition we cannot afford to ignore this description of the fundamental imposture which sustains it.

Translator's Note

In translating from the French, I have chosen for the most part to follow the predominant English usage of the masculine pronoun in cases where gender was grammatically determined in the original. My early attempt to correct this throughout by the consistent use of 'he/she', 'his/her', or of 'she/her' alone, produced either an equality or a 'supremacy' of the feminine term, the absence of which this book attempts to analyse and expose. Within this limit, however, wherever it was possible to use 'he/she' as the acknowledged reference to male and female subjects, I have done so.

Terms like *signifiance* and *jouissance*, for which there are no equivalents in English, and the *objet petit a* (object small a), which is intended to function much as an algebraic sign, have been left in the original in the translated texts in order to allow their meaning to develop from the way in which they operate. They are discussed in the second part of the introduction.

It should be noted that this collection is made up of articles from different sources which were originally presented in a variety of contexts – as papers presented to conferences by Lacan, as part of the seminars which he conducted in Paris between 1953 and 1980, and as articles written by other analysts explicitly for his journal. I have made no attempt to give a false homogeneity to the very divergent styles which follow from this deliberate selection.

Each translation is preceded by a brief statement (in italics) introducing the article and placing it in context for the reader.

J. R.

CHAPTER ONE
Intervention on Transference

Presented to the Congress of Romance-language psychoanalysts in 1951, 'Intervention on Transference' emerged out of Lacan's seminar on Freud's first full-length case-study of an hysterical patient ('Dora', Freud, VII, 1905), which he conducted when he was a member of the Société psychanalytique de Paris. *It was published in the* Revue française de psychanalyse, *the journal of the Society, in 1952.*

The article is a perfect example of that return to, and critical re-reading of, Freud's works which is characteristic of Lacan's work as a whole. It also represents a decisive moment in French psychoanalytic history, in that it was Lacan's insistence that such critical investigation should have a central place in analytic training, separate from the administrative section of the Society, which was one of the precipitating factors behind the split in the Society in 1953. Lacan, together with a number of analysts, resigned in that year, and founded the Société française de psychanalyse *under the presidency of Daniel Lagache.*

Lacan engages here, therefore, with the institution of psychoanalysis — critically, and at a number of different levels. Firstly, in his development of the concept of the ego, *of both analyst and patient, which he identifies as the point of resistance to the analytic treatment, against those theories which see the integration of the* ego *as the objective of the psychoanalytic process. And secondly, in his re-opening of a case, in which the demands of the analyst (here, Freud himself) can be seen to block the treatment at the crucial point of its encounter with the problem of sexual identity.*

The article is important for our purposes in that it immediately raises the problem of femininity as an issue which goes beyond the normative expectations of the analyst. It also calls into question the way psychoanalysis is instituted by revealing the irreducible difficulty, or impasse, of the intersubjective dialogue within which its clinical practice operates.

'Intervention on Transference' was published in Lacan's Ecrits *(Lacan, 1966, pp. 215–26).*

The objective of the present article is once again to accustom people's ears to the term subject. The person providing us with this opportunity will remain anonymous, which will avoid my having to refer to all the passages clearly distinguishing him in what follows.

Had one wished to consider as closed the question of Freud's part in the case of Dora, then there might be an overall advantage to be gained from this attempt to re-open the study of transference, on the appearance of the report presented under that title by Daniel Lagache.[1] His originality was to account for it by means of the Zeigarnik effect,[2] an idea which was bound to please at a time when psychoanalysis seemed to be short of alibis.

When the colleague, who shall be nameless, took the credit of replying to the author of the report that one could equally well claim the presence of transference within this effect, I took this as an opportune moment to talk of psychoanalysis.

I have had to go back on this, since I was moreover way in advance here of what I have stated since on the subject of transference.

By commenting that the Zeigarnik effect would seem more to depend on transference than to be determinant of it, our colleague B introduced what might be called the facts of resistance into the psychotechnic experiment. Their import is the full weight which they give to the primacy of the relationship of subject to subject in all reactions of the individual, inasmuch as these are human, and to the predominance of this relationship in any test of individual dispositions, whether the conditions of that test be defined as a task or a situation.

What needs to be understood as regards psychoanalytic experience is that it proceeds entirely in this relationship of subject to subject, which means that it preserves a dimension which is irreducible to all psychology considered as the objectification of certain properties of the individual.

What happens in an analysis is that the subject is, strictly speaking, constituted through a discourse, to which the mere presence of the psychoanalyst brings, before any intervention, the dimension of dialogue.

Whatever irresponsibility, or even incoherence, the ruling

conventions might come to impose on the principle of this discourse, it is clear that these are merely strategies of navigation (see the case of 'Dora', p. 16)[3] intended to ensure the crossing of certain barriers, and that this discourse must proceed according to the laws of a gravitation, peculiar to it, which is called truth. For 'truth' is the name of that ideal movement which discourse introduces into reality. Briefly, *psychoanalysis is a dialectical experience*, and this notion should predominate when posing the question of the nature of transference.

In this sense my sole objective will be to show, by means of an example, the kind of propositions to which this line of argument might lead. I will, however, first allow myself a few remarks which strike me as urgent for the present guidance of our work of theoretical elaboration, remarks which concern the responsibilities conferred on us by the moment of history we are living, no less than by the tradition entrusted to our keeping.

The fact that a dialectical conception of psychoanalysis has to be presented as an orientation peculiar to my thinking, must, surely, indicate a failure to recognise an immediate given, that is, the self-evident fact that it deals solely with words. While the privileged attention paid to the function of the mute aspects of behaviour in the psychological manoeuvre merely demonstrates a preference on the part of the analyst for a point of view from which the subject is no more than an object. If, indeed, there be such a mis-recognition, then we must question it according to the methods which we would apply in any similar case.

It is known that I am given to thinking that at the moment when the perspective of psychology, together with that of all the human sciences, was thrown into total upheaval by the conceptions originating from psychoanalysis (even if this was without their consent or even their knowledge), then an inverse movement appeared to take place among analysts which I would express in the following terms.

Whereas Freud took it upon himself to show us that there are illnesses which speak (unlike Hesiod, for whom the illnesses sent by Zeus descended on mankind in silence) and to convey the truth of what they are saying, it seems that as the relationship of this truth to a moment in history and a crisis of institutions becomes clearer, so the greater the fear which it inspires in the practitioners who perpetuate its technique.

Thus, in any number of forms, ranging from pious sentiment

to ideals of the crudest efficiency, through the whole gamut of naturalist propaedeutics, they can be seen sheltering under the wing of a psychologism which, in its reification of the human being, could lead to errors besides which those of the physician's scientism would be mere trifles.

For precisely on account of the strength of the forces opened up by analysis, nothing less than a new type of alienation of man is coming into being, as much through the efforts of collective belief as through the selective process of techniques with all the formative weight belonging to rituals: in short, a *homo psychologicus*, which is a danger I would warn you against.

It is in relation to him that I ask you whether we will allow ourselves to be fascinated by his fabrication or whether, by re-thinking the work of Freud, we cannot retrieve the authentic meaning of his initiative and the way to maintain its beneficial value.

Let me stress here, should there be any need, that these questions are in no sense directed at the work of someone like our friend Lagache: the prudence of his method, his scrupulous procedure and the openness of his conclusions, are all exemplary of the distance between our *praxis* and psychology. I will base my demonstration on the case of Dora, because of what it stands for in the experience of transference when this experience was still new, this being the first case in which Freud recognised that the analyst[4] played his part.

It is remarkable that up to now nobody has stressed that the case of Dora is set out by Freud in the form of a series of dialectical reversals. This is not a mere contrivance for presenting material whose emergence Freud clearly states here is left to the will of the patient. What is involved is a scansion of structures in which truth is transmuted for the subject, affecting not only her comprehension of things, but her very position as subject of which her 'objects' are a function. This means that the conception of the case-history is *identical* to the progress of the subject, that is, to the reality of the treatment.

Now, this is the first time Freud gives the term of transference as the concept for the obstacle on which the analysis broke down. This alone gives at the very least the value of a return to sources to the examination I will be conducting of the dialectical relations which constituted the moment of failure. Through this examination, I will be attempting *to define in terms of pure dialectics the transference*, which we call negative on the part of the subject as being the operation of the analyst who interprets it.

We will, however, have to go through all the phases which led up to this moment, while also tracing through them all the problematic insights which, in the given facts of the case, indicate at what points it might have had a successful outcome. Thus we find:

A first development, which is exemplary in that it carries us straight onto the plane where truth asserts itself. Thus, having tested Freud out to see if he will show himself to be as hypocritical as the paternal figure, Dora enters into her indictment, opening up a dossier of memories whose rigour contrasts with the lack of biographical precision which is characteristic of neurosis. Frau K and her father have been lovers for years, concealing the fact with what are at times ridiculous fictions. But what crowns it all is that Dora is thus left defenceless to the attentions of Herr K, to which her father turns a blind eye, thus making her the object of an odious exchange.

Freud is too wise to the consistency of the social lie to have been duped by it, even from the mouth of a man whom he considers owing to him a total confidence. He therefore had no difficulty in removing from the mind of the patient any imputation of complicity over this lie. But at the end of this development he is faced with the question, which is moreover classical in the first stage of a treatment: 'This is all perfectly correct and true, isn't it? What do you want to change in it?' To which Freud's reply is:

A first dialectical reversal which wants nothing of the Hegelian analysis of the protest of the 'beautiful soul', which rises up against the world in the name of the law of the heart: 'Look at your own involvement', he tells her, 'in the disorder which you bemoan' (p. 36).[5] What then appears is:

A second development of truth: namely, that it is not only on the basis of her silence, but through the complicity of Dora herself, and, what is more, even under her vigilant protection, that the fiction had been able to continue which allowed the relationship of the two lovers to carry on. What can be seen here is not simply Dora's participation in the courtship of which she is the object on the part of Herr K. New light is thrown on her relationship to the other partners of the quadrille by the fact that it is caught up in a subtle circulation of precious gifts, serving to compensate the deficiency in sexual services, a circulation which starts with her father in relation to Frau K, and then comes back to the patient through the liberality which it releases in Herr K. Not that this stands in the way of the lavish generosity which comes to her directly from the first source, by way of parallel gifts, this being the classic form of honorable redress through which the bourgeois male has managed to combine the reparation due to the legitimate wife with concern for the patrimony (note that the presence of the wife is reduced here to this lateral appendage to the circuit of exchange).

At the same time it is revealed that Dora's Oedipal relation is grounded in an identification with her father, which is favoured by the latter's sexual impotence and is, moreover, felt by Dora as a reflection on the weight of his position as a man of fortune. This is betrayed by the unconscious allusion which Dora is allowed by the semantics of the word 'fortune' in German: *Vermögen*. As it happens, this identification showed through all the symptoms of conversion presented by Dora, a large number of which were removed by this discovery.

The question then becomes: in the light of this, what is the meaning of the jealousy which Dora suddenly shows towards her father's love affair? The fact that this jealousy presents itself in such a *supervalent* form, calls for an explanation which goes beyond its apparent motives (pp. 54–5).[6] Here takes place:

The second dialectical reversal which Freud brings about by commenting that, far from the alleged object of jealousy providing its true motive, it conceals an interest in the person of the subject–rival, an interest whose nature being much less easily assimilated to common discourse, can only be expressed within it in this inverted form. This gives rise to:

A third development of truth: the fascinated attachment of Dora for Frau K ('her adorable white body', p. 61[7]) the extent to which Dora was confided in, up to a point which will remain unfathomed, on the state of her relations with her husband, the blatant fact of their exchange of friendly services, which they undertook like the joint ambassadoresses of their desires in relation to Dora's father.

Freud spotted the question to which this new development was leading.

If, therefore, it is the loss of this woman that you feel so bitterly, how come you do not resent her for the additional betrayal that it was she who gave rise to those imputations of intrigue and perversity in which they are all now united in accusing you of lying? What is the motive for this loyalty which makes you hold back the last secret of your relationship? (that is, the sexual initiation, readily discernable behind the very accusations of Frau K). It is this secret which brings us:

To the third dialectical reversal, the one which would yield to us the real value of the object which Frau K is for Dora. That is, not an individual, but a mystery, the mystery of her femininity, by which I mean her bodily femininity – as it appears uncovered in the second of the two dreams whose study makes up the second part of Dora's case-history, dreams which I suggest you refer to in order to see how far their interpretation is simplified by my commentary.

The boundary post which we must go round in order to complete the final reversal of our course already appears within reach. It is that most distant of images which Dora retrieves from her early childhood (note that the keys always fall into Freud's hands even in those cases which are broken off like this one). The image is that of Dora, probably still an *infans*, sucking her left thumb, while with her right hand she tugs at the ear of her brother, her elder by a year and a half (p. 51 and p. 21).[8]

What we seem to have here is the imaginary matrix in which all the situations developed by Dora during her life have since come to be cast – a perfect illustration of the theory of repetition compulsion, which was yet to appear in Freud's work. It gives us the measure of what woman and man signify for her now.

Woman is the object which it is impossible to detach from a primitive oral desire, and yet in which she must learn to recognise her own genital nature. (One wonders here why Freud fails to see that the aphonia brought on during the absences of Herr K (pp. 39–40)[9] is an expression of the violent appeal of the oral erotic drive when Dora was left face to face with Frau K, without there being any need for him to invoke her awareness of the *fellatio* undergone by the father (pp. 47–8),[10] when everyone knows that cunnilingus is the artifice most commonly adopted by 'men of means' whose powers begin to abandon them.) In order for her to gain access to this recognition of her femininity, she would have to take on this assumption of her own body, failing which she remains open to that functional fragmentation (to refer to the theoretical contribution of the mirror stage), which constitutes conversion symptoms.

Now, if she was to fulfil the condition for this access, the original *imago* shows us that her only opening to the object was through the intermediary of the masculine partner, with whom, because of the slight difference in years, she was able to identify, in that primordial identification through which the subject recognises itself as *I* . . . .

So Dora had identified with Herr K, just as she is in the process of identifying with Freud himself. (The fact that it was on waking from her dream 'of transference' that Dora noticed the smell of smoke belonging to the two men does not indicate, as Freud said (p. 73),[11] a more deeply repressed identification, but much more that this hallucination corresponded to the dawning of her reversion to the *ego*.) And all her dealings with the two men manifest that aggressivity which is the dimension characteristic of narcissistic alienation.

Thus it is the case, as Freud thinks, that the return to a passionate outburst against the father represents a regression as regards the relationship started up with Herr K.

But this homage, whose beneficial value for Dora is sensed by Freud, could be received by her as a manifestation of desire only if she herself could accept herself as an object of desire, that is to say, only once she had worked out the meaning of what she was searching for in Frau K.

As is true for all women, and for reasons which are at the very basis of the most elementary forms of social exchange (the very reasons which Dora gives as the grounds for her revolt), the problem of her condition is fundamentally that of accepting herself as an object of desire for the man, and this is for Dora the mystery which motivates her idolatry for Frau K. Just as in her long meditation before the Madonna, and in her recourse to the role of distant worshipper, Dora is driven towards the solution which Christianity has given to this subjective impasse, by making woman the object of a divine desire, or else, a transcendant object of desire, which amounts to the same thing.

If, therefore, in a third dialectical reversal, Freud had directed Dora towards a recognition of what Frau K was for her, by getting her to confess the last secrets of their relationship, then what would have been his prestige (this merely touches on the meaning of positive transference) – thereby opening up the path to a recognition of the virile object? This is not my opinion, but that of Freud (p. 120).[12]

But the fact that his failure to do so was fatal to the treatment, is attributed by Freud to the action of the transference (pp. 116–20),[13] to his error in putting off its interpretation (p. 118),[14] when, as he was able to ascertain after the fact, he had only two hours before him in which to avoid its effects (p. 119).[15]

But each time he comes back to invoking this explanation (one whose subsequent development in analytic doctrine is well known), a note at the foot of the page goes and adds an appeal to his insufficient appreciation of the homosexual tie binding Dora to Frau K.

What this must mean is that the second reason only strikes him as the most crucial in 1923, whereas the first bore fruit in his thinking from 1905, the date when Dora's case-study was published.

As for us, which side should we come down on? Surely that of crediting him on both counts by attempting to grasp what can be deduced from their synthesis.

What we then find is this. Freud admits that for a long time he was unable to face this homosexual tendency (which he none the less tells us is so constant in hysterics that its subjective role cannot be overestimated) without falling into a perplexity (p. 120, n. 1)[16] which made him incapable of dealing with it satisfactorily.

We would say that this has to be ascribed to prejudice, exactly the same prejudice which falsifies the conception of the Oedipus complex from the start, by making it define as natural, rather than normative, the predominance of the paternal figure. This is the same prejudice which we hear expressed simply in the well-known refrain 'As thread to needle, so girl to boy.'

Freud feels a sympathy for Herr K which goes back a long way, since it was Herr K that brought Dora's father to Freud (p. 19)[17] and this comes out in numerous appreciative remarks (p. 29, n. 3).[18] After the breakdown of the treatment, Freud persists in dreaming of a 'triumph of love' (pp. 109–10).[19]

As regards Dora, Freud admits his personal involvement in the interest which she inspires in him at many points in the account. The truth of the matter is that it sets the whole case on an edge which, breaking through the theoretical digression, elevates this text, among the psychopathological monographs which make up a genre of our literature, to the tone of a *Princesse de Clèves* trapped by a deadly blocking of utterance.[20]

It is because he put himself rather too much in the place of Herr K that, this time, Freud did not succeed in moving the Acheron.

Due to his counter-transference, Freud keeps reverting to the love which Herr K might have inspired in Dora, and it is odd to see how he always interprets as though they were confessions what are in fact the very varied responses which Dora argues against him. The session when he thinks he has reduced her to 'no longer contradicting him' (p. 104)[21] and which he feels able to end by expressing to her his satisfaction, Dora in fact concludes on a very different note. 'Why, has anything so very remarkable come out?' she says, and it is at the start of the following session that she takes her leave of him.

What, therefore, happened during the scene of the declaration at the lakeside, the catastrophe upon which Dora entered her illness, leading on everyone to recognise her as ill – this, ironically, being their response to her refusal to carry on as the prop for their common infirmity (not all the 'gains' of a neurosis work solely to the advantage of the neurotic)?

As in any valid interpretation, we need only stick to the text in order to understand it. Herr K could only get in a few words, decisive though they were: 'My wife is nothing to me.' The reward for his effort was instantaneous: a hard slap (whose burning after-effects Dora felt long after the treatment in the form of a transitory neuralgia) gave back to the blunderer – 'If she is nothing to you, then what are you to me?'

And after that what will he be for her, this puppet who has none the less just broken the enchantment under which she had been living for years?

The latent pregnancy fantasy which follows on from this scene cannot be argued against our interpretation, since it is a well-known fact that it occurs in hysterics precisely as a function of their virile identification.

It is through the very same trap door that Freud will disappear, in a sliding which is even more insidious. Dora withdraws with the smile of the *Mona Lisa* and even when she reappears, Freud is not so naive as to believe her intention is to return.

At this moment she has got everyone to recognise the truth which, while it may be truthful, she knows does not constitute the final truth, and she then manages through the mere *mana* of her presence to precipitate the unfortunate Herr K under the wheels of a carriage. The subduing of her symptoms, which had been brought about during the second phase of the treatment, did however last. Thus the arrest of the dialectical process is sealed by an obvious retreat, but the positions reverted to can only be sustained by an assertion of the *ego*, which can be taken as an improvement.

Finally, therefore, what is this transference whose work Freud states somewhere goes on invisibly behind the progress of the treatment, and whose effects, furthermore, are 'not susceptible to definite proof' (p. 74)?[22] Surely in this case it can be seen as an entity altogether relative to the counter-transference, defined as the sum total of the prejudices, passions and difficulties of the analyst, or even of his insufficient information, at any given moment of the dialectical process. Doesn't Freud himself tell us (p. 118)[23] that Dora might have transferred onto him the paternal figure, had he been fool enough to believe in the version of things which the father had presented to him?

In other words, the transference is nothing real in the subject other than the appearance, in a moment of stagnation of the analytic dialectic, of the permanent modes according to which it constitutes its objects.

What, therefore, is meant by interpreting the transference? Nothing other than a ruse to fill in the emptiness of this deadlock. But while it may be deceptive, this ruse serves a purpose by setting off the whole process again.

Thus, even though Dora would have denied any suggestion of Freud's that she was imputing to him the same intentions as had been displayed by Herr K, this would in no sense have reduced its effectivity. The very opposition to which it would have given rise would probably, despite Freud, have set Dora off in the favourable direction: that which would have led her to the object of her real interest.

And the fact of setting himself up personally as a substitute for Herr K would have saved Freud from over-insisting on the value of the marriage proposals of the latter.

Thus transference does not arise from any mysterious property of affectivity, and even when it reveals an emotive aspect, this only has meaning as a function of the dialectical moment in which it occurs.

But this moment is of no great significance since it normally translates an error on the part of the analyst, if only that of wishing too much for the good of the patient, a danger Freud warned against on many occasions.

Thus analytic neutrality takes its true meaning from the position of the pure dialectician who, knowing that all that is real is rational (and vice versa), knows that all that exists, including the evil against which he struggles, corresponds as it always will to the level of his own particularity, and that there is no progress for the subject other than through the integration which he arrives at from his position in the universal: technically through the projection of his past into a discourse in the process of becoming.

The case of Dora is especially relevant for this demonstration in that, since it involves an hysteric, the screen of the *ego* is fairly transparent – there being nowhere else, as Freud has said, where the threshold is lower between the unconscious and the conscious, or rather, between the analytic discourse and the *word* of the symptom.

I believe, however, that transference always has this same meaning of indicating the moments where the analyst goes astray, and equally takes his or her bearings, this same value of calling us back to the order of our role – that of a positive non-acting with a view to the ortho-dramatisation of the subjectivity of the patient.

Notes

1. Daniel Lagache, 'Some Aspects of Transference', *IJPA*, XXXIV, 1 (1953), pp. 1–10 (tr.).
2. Briefly, this consists of the psychological effect produced by an unfinished task when it leaves a *Gestalt* in suspense: for instance, that of the generally felt need to give to a musical bar its rhyming chord.
3. *Pelican Freud* (vol. 8), p. 45 (see note 4).
4. So that the reader can check my commentary in its textual detail, wherever I refer to Freud's case study, reference is given to *Denoël's Edition* in the text, and to the 1954 *P.U.F.* in a footnote. (*Standard Edition* vol. VII, and *Pelican Freud,* vol. 8 (tr.)).
5. *Pelican Freud* (vol. 8), p. 67.
6. Ibid., p. 88–9.
7. Ibid., p. 96.
8. Ibid., p. 85 and p. 51.
9. Ibid., pp. 71–2.
10. Ibid., pp. 80–1.
11. Ibid., p. 109.

12. Ibid., p. 162.
13. Ibid., pp. 157–62.
14. Ibid., p. 160.
15. Ibid., p. 161.
16. Ibid., p. 162, n. 1.
17. Ibid., p. 49.
18. Ibid., p. 60, n. 2.
19. Ibid., pp. 151–2.
20. *La Princesse de Clèves*, Madame de Lafayette (Paris: Claude Barbin, 1678). This novel has always had in France the status of a classic. What is relevant here is that (a) it is taken up almost entirely with the account of a love which is socially and morally unacceptable; and (b) in the decisive moment of the plot, the heroine confesses to her husband, who, previously a model of moral generosity, is destroyed by the revelation (tr.).
21. *Pelican Freud*, p. 145.
22. Ibid., p. 110.
23. Ibid., p. 160.

CHAPTER TWO
The Meaning of the Phallus

'The Meaning of the Phallus' is the only article of this collection previously to have appeared in English. It is included as Lacan's most direct exposition of the status of the phallus in the psychoanalytic account of sexuality. This is the issue around which the whole controversy over femininity has turned.

It was first presented in German at the Max Planck Institute in Munich in 1958. At this stage, Lacan was concerned above all to emphasise the place of the symbolic order in the determination of human subjectivity, and to give an account of that order in terms of the laws of linguistic operation – the contemporary science of linguistics, as he argues here, having been unavailable to Freud.

Lacan, therefore, returns to the debates of the 1920s and 1930s (Abraham, Jones, Klein) and criticises what he sees as a reduction of the phallus to an object of primitive oral aggression, belonging in the realm of the instinct. Instead he places the phallus within the symbolic order, and argues that it can only be understood as a signifier in the linguistic sense of the term.

This is the first article of this collection to introduce the central concept of desire, which indicates for Lacan the fundamental division which characterises the subject's relation to language, a dimension which he felt was avoided in discussion of the genital relation in certain French analytic circles at that time. Lacan, on the other hand, traces his conception through to the difficulties of the sexual relation itself, especially – we would stress – for the woman, whose relationship to the phallic term is described essentially in terms of masquerade.

This is perhaps the article which illustrates most clearly the problem of giving an explanation of the phallus which avoids reducing it to the biological difference between the sexes, but which none the less tries to provide a differential account, for men and for women, of its effects.

'The Meaning of the Phallus' was published in Ecrits (pp. 685–95), and translated by Alan Sheridan as 'The Signification of the Phallus' in Ecrits: a Selection (Lacan, 1977, pp. 281–91). The following text is a new translation for this collection.

What follows is the unaltered text of a paper delivered in German on 9 May 1958, at the Max Planck Institute of Munich where Professor Paul Matussek had invited me to speak.

The vaguest idea of the state of mind then prevailing in circles, not for the most part uninformed, will give some measure of the impact of terms such as 'the other scene', to take one example used here, which I was the first to extract from Freud's work.

If 'deferred action' (*Nachtrag*), to rescue another such term from its current affectation, makes this effort unfeasible, it should be realised that they were unheard of at that time.

We know that the unconscious castration complex has the function of a knot:

(1) in the dynamic structuring of symptoms in the analytic sense of the term, meaning that which can be analysed in neuroses, perversions and psychoses;
(2) as the regulator of development giving its *ratio* to this first role: that is, by installing in the subject an unconscious position without which he would be unable to identify with the ideal type of his sex, or to respond without grave risk to the needs of his partner in the sexual relation, or even to receive adequately the needs of the child thus procreated.

What we are dealing with is an antinomy internal to the assumption by man (*Mensch*) of his sex: why must he take up its attributes only by means of a threat, or even in the guise of a privation? As we know, in *Civilisation and its Discontents*, Freud went so far as to suggest not a contingent, but an essential disturbance of human sexuality, and one of his last articles turns on the irreducibility for any finite (*endliche*) analysis of the effects following from the castration complex in the masculine unconscious and from *penisneid* [penis envy] in the unconscious of the woman.

This is not the only point of uncertainty, but it is the first that the Freudian experience and its resulting metapsychology introduced into our experience of man. It cannot be solved by any reduction to biological factors, as the mere necessity of the myth underlying the structuring of the Oedipus complex makes sufficiently clear.

Any recourse to an hereditary amnesic given would in this instance be mere artifice, not only because such a factor is in itself disputable, but because it leaves the problem untouched, namely, the link between the murder of the father and the pact of the primordial law, given that it is included in that law that castration should be the punishment for incest.

Only on the basis of the clinical facts can there be any fruitful discussion. These facts go to show that the relation of the subject to the phallus is set up regardless of the anatomical difference between the sexes, which is what makes its interpretation particularly intractable in the case of the woman and in relationship to her, specifically on the four following counts:

(1) as to why the little girl herself considers, if only for a moment, that she is castrated, in the sense of being deprived of the phallus, at the hand of someone who is in the first instance her mother, an important point, and who then becomes her father, but in such a way that we must recognise in this transition a transference in the analytic sense of the term;

(2) as to why, at a more primordial level, the mother is for both sexes considered as provided with a phallus, that is, as a phallic mother;

(3) as to why, correlatively, the meaning of castration only acquires its full (clinically manifest) weight as regards symptom formation when it is discovered as castration of the mother;

(4) these three problems culminate in the question of the reason for the phallic phase in development. We know that Freud used this term to specify the earliest genital maturation – as on the one hand characterised by the imaginary predominance of the phallic attribute and masturbatory pleasure, and on the other by a localising of this pleasure for the woman in the clitoris, which is thereby raised to the function of the phallus. This would seem to rule out for both sexes, until the end of this phase, that is, until the dissolution of the Oedipus complex, any instinctual awareness of the vagina as the place of genital penetration.

This ignorance smacks of mis-recognition [*méconnaissance*] in the technical sense of the term, especially as it is on occasions disproved. All it agrees with, surely, is Longus's fable in which he depicts the initiation of Daphnis and Chloë as dependent on the revelations of an old woman.

It is for this reason that certain authors have been led to regard the phallic phase as an effect of repression, and the function assumed in it by the phallic object as a symptom. The difficulty starts when we need to know *which* symptom? Phobia, according to one, perversion according to another – or, indeed, to the same one. In this last case, it's not worth speculating: not that interesting transmutations of the object from phobia into fetish do not occur, but their interest resides precisely in the different place which they occupy in the structure. There would be no point in asking these authors to formulate this difference from the perspective of object relations which is currently in favour. This being for lack of any reference on the matter other than the loose notion of the part object, uncriticised since Karl Abraham first introduced it, which is more the pity in view of the easy option which it provides today.

The fact remains that, if one goes back to the surviving texts of the years 1928–32, the now abandoned debate on the phallic phase is a refreshing example of a passion for doctrine, which has been given an additional note of nostalgia by the degradation of psychoanalysis consequent on its American transplantation.

A mere summary of the debate could only distort the genuine diversity of the positions taken by figures such as Helene Deutsch, Karen Horney and Ernest Jones, to mention only the most eminent.

The series of three articles which Jones devoted to the subject is especially suggestive: if only for the starting premise on which he constructs his argument, signalled by the term *aphanisis*, which he himself coined. For by correctly posing the problem of the relationship between castration and desire, he reveals such a proximity to what he cannot quite grasp that the term which will later provide us with the key to the problem seems to emerge out of his very failure.

The amusing thing is the way he manages, on the authority of the very letter of Freud's text, to formulate a position which is directly opposed to it: a true model in a difficult genre.

The problem, however, refuses to go away, seeming to subvert Jones's own case for a re-establishment of the equality of natural rights (which surely gets the better of him in the Biblical 'Man and woman God created them' with which he concludes).

What does he actually gain by normalising the function of the phallus as part object if he has to invoke its presence in the mother's body as internal object, a term which is a function of the fantasies uncovered by Melanie Klein, and if he cannot therefore separate himself from her doctrine which sees these fantasies as a recurrence of the Oedipal formation which is located right back in earliest infancy.

We will not go far wrong if we re-open the question by asking what could have imposed on Freud the obvious paradox of his position. For one has to allow that he was better guided than anyone else in his recognition of the order of unconscious phenomena, which order he had discovered, and that for want of an adequate articulation of the nature of these phenomena his followers were bound to go more or less astray.

It is on the basis of such a wager – laid down by me as the principle of a commentary of Freud's work which I have been pursuing for seven years – that I have been led to certain conclusions: above all, to argue, as necessary to any articulation of analytic phenomena, for the notion of the signifier, in the sense in which it is opposed to that of the signified in modern linguistic analysis. The latter, born since Freud, could not be taken into account by him, but it is my contention that Freud's discovery stands out precisely for having had to anticipate its formulas, even while setting out from a domain in which one could hardly expect to recognise its sway. Conversely, it is Freud's discovery that gives to the opposition of signifier to signified the full weight which it should imply: namely, that the signifier has an active function in determining the effects in which the signifiable appears as submitting to its mark, becoming through that passion the signified.

This passion of the signifier then becomes a new dimension of the human condition, in that it is not only man who speaks, but in man and through man that it [*ça*] speaks, that his nature is woven by effects in which we can find the structure of language, whose material he becomes, and that consequently there resounds in him, beyond anything ever conceived of by the psychology of ideas, the relation of speech.

It is in this sense that one can say that the consequences of the discovery of the unconscious have not been so much as glimpsed in the theory, although its repercussions have been felt in the praxis to a much greater extent than we are as yet aware of, even if only translated into effects of retreat.

Let me make clear that to argue for man's relation to the signifier as such has nothing to do with a 'culturalist' position in the ordinary sense of the term, such as that which Karen Horney found herself anticipating in the dispute over the phallus and which Freud himself characterised as feminist. The issue is not man's relation to language as a social phenomenon, since the question does not even arise of anything resembling that all too familiar ideological psychogenesis, not superseded by a peremptory recourse to the entirely metaphysical notion, underlying the mandatory appeal to the concrete, which is so pathetically conveyed by the term 'affect'.

It is a question of rediscovering in the laws governing that other scene (*eine andere Schauplatz*) which Freud designated, in relation to dreams, as that of the unconscious, the effects discovered at the level of the materially unstable elements which constitute the chain of language: effects determined by the double play of combination and substitution in the signifier, along the two axes of metaphor and metonymy which generate the signified; effects which are determinant in the institution of the subject. What emerges from this attempt is a topology in the mathematical sense of the term, without which, as soon becomes clear, it is impossible even to register the structure of a symptom in the analytic sense of the term.

It speaks in the Other, I say, designating by this Other the very place called upon by a recourse to speech in any relation where it intervenes. If it speaks in the Other, whether or not the subject hears it with his own ears, it is because it is there that the subject, according to a logic prior to any awakening of the signified, finds his signifying place. The discovery of what he articulates in that place, that is, in the unconscious, enables us to grasp the price of the division (*Spaltung*) through which he is thus constituted.

The phallus is elucidated in its function here. In Freudian doctrine, the phallus is not a fantasy, if what is understood by that is an imaginary effect. Nor is it as such an object (part, internal, good, bad, etc. . . .) in so far as this term tends to accentuate the reality involved in a relationship. It is even less the organ, penis or clitoris, which it symbolises. And it is not incidental that Freud took his reference for it from the simulacrum which it represented for the Ancients.

For the phallus is a signifier, a signifier whose function in the intrasubjective economy of analysis might lift the veil from that which it served in the mysteries. For it is to this signified that it is given to designate as a whole the effect of there being a signified, inasmuch as it conditions any such effect by its presence as signifier.

Let us examine, then, the effects of this presence. First they follow from the deviation of man's needs by the fact that he speaks, in the sense that as long as his needs are subjected to demand they return to him alienated. This is not the effect of his real dependency (one should not expect to find here the parasitic conception represented by the notion of dependency in the theory of neuroses) but precisely of the putting into signifying form as such and of the fact that it is from the place of the Other that his message is emitted.

What is thus alienated in needs constitutes an *Urverdrängung* (primal repression) because it cannot, by definition, be articulated in demand. But it reappears in a residue which then presents itself in man as desire (*das Begehren*). The phenomenology which emerges from analytic experience is certainly such as to demonstrate the paradoxical, deviant, erratic, excentric and even scandalous character by which desire is distinguished from need. A fact too strongly attested not to have always won the recognition of moralists worthy of the name. It does seem that early Freudianism had to give this fact its due status. Yet paradoxically psychoanalysis finds itself at the head of an age-old obscurantism, all the more wearisome for its denial of the fact through the ideal of a theoretical and practical reduction of desire to need.

Hence the necessity for us to articulate that status here, starting with demand whose proper characteristics are eluded in the notion of frustration (which was never employed by Freud).

Demand in itself bears on something other than the satisfactions which it calls for. It is demand for a presence or an absence. This is manifest in the primordial relation to the mother, pregnant as it is with that Other to be situated *some way short of* any needs which it might gratify. Demand constitutes this Other as already possessing the 'privilege' of satisfying needs, that is, the power to deprive them of the one thing by which they are satisfied. This privilege of the Other thus sketches out the radical form of the gift of something which it does not have, namely, what is called its love.

Hence it is that demand cancels out (*aufhebt*) the particularity of anything which might be granted by transmuting it into a proof of love, and the very satisfactions of need which it obtains are degraded (*sich erniedrigt*) as being no more than a crushing of the demand for love (all of which is palpable in the psychology of early child-care to which our nurse-analysts are so dedicated).

There is, then, a necessity for the particularity thus abolished to reappear *beyond* demand. Where it does indeed reappear, but preserving the structure harbouring within the unconditional character of the demand for love. In a reversal which is not a simple negation of negation, the force of pure loss arises from the relic of an obliteration. In place of the unconditional aspect of demand, desire substitutes the 'absolute' condition: in effect this condition releases that part of the proof of love which is resistant to the satisfaction of a need. Thus desire is neither the appetite for satisfaction, nor the demand for love, but the difference resulting from the subtraction of the first from the second, the very phenomenon of their splitting (*Spaltung*).

One can see how the sexual relation occupies this closed field of desire in which it will come to play out its fate. For this field is constituted so as to produce the enigma which this relation provokes in the subject, by 'signifying' it to him twice over: as a return of the demand it arouses in the form of a demand made on the subject of need, and as an ambiguity cast onto the Other who is involved, in the proof of love demanded. The gap in this enigma betrays what determines it, conveyed at its simplest in this formula: that for each partner in the relation, the subject and the Other, it is not enough to be the subjects of need, nor objects of love, but they must stand as the cause of desire.

This truth is at the heart of all the mishaps of sexual life which belong in the field of psychoanalysis.

It is also the precondition in analysis for the subject's happiness: and to disguise this gap by relying on the virtue of the 'genital' to resolve it through the maturation of tenderness (that is by a recourse to the Other solely as reality), however piously intended, is none the less a fraud. Admittedly it was French psychoanalysts with their hypocritical notion of genital oblativity who started up the moralising trend which, to the tune of Salvationist choirs, is now followed everywhere.

In any case man cannot aim at being whole (the 'total personality' being another premise where modern psychotherapy goes off course) once the play of displacement and condensation, to which he is committed in the exercise of his functions, marks his relation as subject to the signifier.

The phallus is the privileged signifier of that mark where the share of the logos is wedded to the advent of desire. One might say that this signifier is chosen as what stands out as most easily seized upon in the real of sexual copulation, and also as the most symbolic in the literal (typographical) sense of the term, since it is the equivalent in that relation of the (logical) copula. One might also say that by virtue of its turgidity, it is the image of the vital flow as it is transmitted in generation.

All these propositions merely veil over the fact that the phallus can only play its role as veiled, that is, as in itself the sign of the latency with which everything signifiable is struck as soon as it is raised (*aufgehoben*) to the function of signifier.

The phallus is the signifier of this *Aufhebung* itself which it inaugurates (initiates) by its own disappearance. This is why the demon of Αἰδώς [*Scham*, shame] in the ancient mysteries rises up exactly at the moment when the phallus is unveiled (cf. the famous painting of the Villa of Pompei).

It then becomes the bar which, at the hands of this demon, strikes the signified, branding it as the bastard offspring of its signifying concatenation.

In this way a condition of complementarity is produced by the signifier in the founding of the subject: which explains his *Spaltung* as well as the intervening movement through which this is effected.
Namely:

(1) that the subject designates his being only by crossing through everything which it signifies, as can be seen in the fact that he wishes to be loved for himself, a mirage not dispelled merely by being denounced as grammatical (since it abolishes discourse);

(2) that the living part of that being in the *urverdrängt* [primary repressed] finds its signifier by receiving the mark of the *Verdrängung* [repression] of the phallus (whereby the unconscious is language).

The phallus as signifier gives the ratio of desire (in the musical sense of the term as the 'mean and extreme' ratio of harmonic division).

It is, therefore, as an algorithm that I am going to use it now, relying – necessarily if I am to avoid drawing out my account indefinitely – on the echoes of the experience which unites us to give you the sense of this usage.

If the phallus is a signifier then it is in the place of the Other that the subject gains access to it. But in that the signifier is only there veiled and as the ratio of the Other's desire, so it is this desire of the Other as such which the subject has to recognise, meaning, the Other as itself a subject divided by the signifying *Spaltung*.

What can be seen to emerge in psychological genesis confirms this signifying function of the phallus.

Thus, to begin with, we can formulate more correctly the Kleinian fact that the child apprehends from the outset that the mother 'contains' the phallus.

But it is the dialectic of the demand for love and the test of desire which dictates the order of development.

The demand for love can only suffer from a desire whose signifier is alien to it. If the desire of the mother *is* the phallus, then the child wishes to be the phallus so as to satisfy this desire. Thus the division immanent to desire already makes itself felt in the desire of the Other, since it stops the subject from being satisfied with presenting to the Other anything real it might *have* which corresponds to this phallus – what he has being worth no more than what he does not have as far as his demand for love is concerned, which requires that he *be* the phallus.

Clinical practice demonstrates that this test of the desire of the Other is not decisive in the sense that the subject learns from it whether or not he has a real phallus, but inasmuch as he learns that the mother does not. This is the moment of experience without which no symptomatic or structural consequence (that is, phobia or *penisneid*) referring to the castration complex can take effect. It is here that the conjunction is signed between desire, in so far as the phallic signifier is its mark, and the threat or the nostalgia of lack-in-having.

It is, of course, the law introduced into this sequence by the father which will decide its future.

But simply by keeping to the function of the phallus, we can pinpoint the structures which will govern the relations between the sexes.

Let us say that these relations will revolve around a being and a having which, because they refer to a signifier, the phallus, have the contradictory effect of on the one hand lending reality to the subject in that signifier, and on the other making unreal the relations to be signified.

This follows from the intervention of an 'appearing' which gets substituted for the 'having' so as to protect it on one side and to mask its lack on the other, with the effect that the ideal or typical manifestations of behaviour in both sexes, up to and including the act of sexual copulation, are entirely propelled into comedy.

These ideals gain new strength from the demand which it is in their power to satisfy, which is always the demand for love, with its complement of reducing desire to demand.

Paradoxical as this formulation might seem, I would say that it is in order to be the phallus, that is to say, the signifier of the desire of the Other, that the woman will reject an essential part of her femininity, notably all its attributes through masquerade. It is for what she is not that she expects to be desired as well as loved. But she finds the signifier of her own desire in the body of the one to whom she addresses her demand for love. Certainly we should not forget that the organ actually invested with this signifying function takes on the value of a fetish. But for the woman the result is still a convergence onto the same object of an experience of love which as such (cf. above) ideally deprives her of that which it gives, and a desire which finds in that same experience its signifier. Which is why it can be observed that the lack of satisfaction proper to sexual need, in other words, frigidity, is relatively well tolerated in women, whereas the *Verdrängung* inherent to desire is lesser in her case than in the case of the man.

In men, on the other hand, the dialectic of demand and desire gives rise to effects, whose exact point of connection Freud situated with a sureness which we must once again admire, under the rubric of a specific depreciation (*Erniedrigung*) of love.

If it is the case that the man manages to satisfy his demand for love in his relationship to the woman to the extent that the signifier of the phallus constitutes her precisely as giving in love what she does not have – conversely, his own desire for the phallus will throw up its signifier in the form of a persistent divergence towards 'another woman' who can signify this phallus under various guises, whether as a virgin or a prostitute. The result is a centrifugal tendency of the genital drive in the sexual life of the man which makes impotence much harder for him to bear, at the same time as the *Verdrängung* inherent to desire is greater.

We should not, however, think that the type of infidelity which then appears to be constitutive of the masculine function is exclusive to the man. For if one looks more closely, the same redoubling is to be found in the woman, except that in her case, the Other of love as such, that is to say, the Other as deprived of that which he gives, is hard to perceive in the withdrawal whereby it is substituted for the being of the man whose attributes she cherishes.

One might add here that masculine homosexuality, in accordance with the phallic mark which constitutes desire, is constituted on its axis, whereas the orientation of feminine homo-sexuality, as observation shows, follows from a disappointment which reinforces the side of the demand for love. These remarks should be qualified by going back to the function of the mask inasmuch as this function dominates the identifications through which refusals of love are resolved.

The fact that femininity takes refuge in this mask, because of the *Verdrängung* inherent to the phallic mark of desire, has the strange consequence that, in the human being, virile display itself appears as feminine.

Correlatively, one can glimpse the reason for a feature which has never been elucidated and which again gives a measure of the depth of Freud's intuition: namely, why he advances the view that there is only one libido, his text clearly indicating that he conceives of it as masculine in nature. The function of the signifier here touches on its most profound relation: by way of which the Ancients embodied in it both the Νοῦς [*Nous*, sense] and the Λογὸς [*Logos*, reason].

CHAPTER THREE

Guiding Remarks for a Congress on Feminine Sexuality

'Guiding Remarks for a Congress on Feminine Sexuality' takes up points of controversy on the specific issue of feminine sexuality, as it appears in clinical practice. It is, therefore, a complement to 'The Meaning of the Phallus'. It was written in the same year, 1958, two years before a Colloquium on feminine sexuality, organised by the Société française de psychanalyse, *which took place at the municipal University of Amsterdam in September 1960.*

The article appeared in 1964 in a special issue (no. 7) of La Psychanalyse *(the journal of the Society) on the question of feminine sexuality. The issue included, together with the papers from the congress, articles by Helene Deutsch (1925), Ernest Jones (1927, 1933) and Joan Rivière (1929), which had formed a central part of the earlier psychoanalytic debate on femininity in the 1920s and 1930s.*

The article is laid out as a series of points, questions addressed to psychoanalysis around those topics – frigidity, masochism, passivity – which have conventionally come to be associated with feminine sexuality. These concepts, in which we can recognise a fully ideological account of femininity, are characterised here by Lacan in terms of mistake, omission and prejudice. Lacan argues that their theorisation by psychoanalysis has for the most part rested ultimately on a recourse to physiology or nature, and that the implications of the concept of the unconscious, in relation to desire and its representations, have been lost. The stress again here is that femininity cannot be understood outside the symbolic process through which it is constituted.

In this article, the problem of femininity is unequivocally the problem of the symbolic articulation of its forms. This raises issues, only touched on at the very end, which go beyond the domain of psychoanalysis proper, to the more familiar instances of women's subordination.

'Guiding Remarks for a Congress on Feminine Sexuality' was published in Ecrits *(pp. 725–36).*

I Historical introduction

Taking the experience of psychoanalysis in its development over sixty years, it comes as no surprise to note that, whereas the first outcome of its origins was a conception of the castration complex based on paternal repression, it has progressively directed its interests towards the frustrations coming from the mother, not that such a distortion has shed any light on the complex.

A notion of emotional deprivation linking disturbances of development directly to the real inadequacies of mothering has been overlaid with a dialectic of fantasies which takes the maternal body as its imaginary field.

What is unquestionably involved here is a conceptual fore-grounding of the sexuality of the woman, which brings to our attention a remarkable oversight.

II Definition of the subject

This is an oversight which bears directly on the issue which I would like to draw your attention to here, namely, that of the feminine part, if the term has any meaning, of what is played out in the genital relation, in which the act of coitus occupies, to put it no higher, a limited and local place.

Or, alternatively, so as not to fall down on the distinguished biological references which continue to gratify: what are the paths of libido laid down for the woman by the anatomical characteristics of sexual differentiation in the higher organisms?

III Reassessment of the facts

Such a project requires first that we reassess:

(a) the phenomena to which women testify within the conditions of psychoanalytic experience in relation to the paths leading to, and the act of, coitus, as confirming or otherwise the nosological bases of our medical point of departure;

(b) the subordination of these phenomena to forces which our practice recognises as desires, especially to their unconscious residues (together with the ensuing effects on the psychic economy whether these be efferent or afferent in relation to the act), amongst which residues those of love can be considered on their own account without prejudicing the transmission of their consequences to the child;

(c) the as yet unchallenged implications of a psychical bi-sexuality which was originally attributed to the duplications of anatomy, but has increasingly been ascribed to the logic of personal identifications.

IV   Glaring omissions

A summary of this kind would bring out certain omissions, whose interest cannot simply be dismissed as 'not proven':

1. On the one hand, recent developments within physiology, such as the fact of chromosomic sexuality and its genetic cor-relates, as distinct from hormonal sexuality, and the relative share of each in anatomical determination; or simply what appears to be a libidinal predominance of the male hormone, to the extent of its regulating the oestrogen metabolism in the menstrual phenomenon. While the clinical interpretations of these facts may still be subject to reservations, yet they demand consideration no less for having been consistently ignored by a practice which would sooner claim messianic access to decisive chemical forces.

The fact of our keeping, here, at a distance from the real may well raise the question of the division deliberately being imposed – which if it does not belong between the somatic and the psychic, which are in fact continuous, should be made between the organism and the subject. This assumes that we repudiate the affective dimension which the theory of error lays on this subject, and articulate it as the subject of a combinatory logic, which alone gives the unconscious its meaning.

2. On the other hand, the key position of the phallus in libidinal development is a paradox exclusive to the psychoanalytic approach, which must be addressed because of its insistent recur-rence in the facts.

This is where the question of the phallic phase for the woman becomes even more problematic, in that having unleashed a fury during the years 1927–35, it has since been left, in a tacit understanding, to the good will of individual interpretation.

Only by asking why this is the case, might we possibly break this deadlock.

When in this instance the terms imaginary, real or symbolic are used to refer to the incidence of the phallus in the subjective structure where development is lodged, they are not the words of a particular teaching, but the very words which signal under the pens of their authors the conceptual slidings which, because they went unchecked, led to the lull experienced after the breakdown of the debate.

V   The obscurity concerning the vaginal organ

However oblique a way of proceeding, noting a prohibition can serve as a prelude.

A prohibition which seems to be confirmed by the fact that psychoanalysis, as a discipline which answered from its field in the name of sexuality, and seemed to be about to bring its whole secret to light, gave up on what can be uncovered about feminine *jouissance* at exactly the same point that a scarcely zealous physiology admits to being licked.

The fairly trivial opposition between clitoral orgasm and vaginal satisfaction has had theory backing its cause, to the point of laying at its door the distress of subjects, and even of turning it into an issue, if not a platform – not that one can say that any light has been shed on the antagonism between the two.

This being because the vaginal orgasm has kept the darkness of its nature inviolate.

For it has been shown that the massotherapeutic notion of the sensitivity of the cervix and the surgical notion of a *noli tangere* of the rear lining of the vagina are contingent factors (doubtless in hysterectomies but also in vaginal aplasias!).

The representatives of the female sex, however loud their voices at the analysts, do not seem to have done their utmost towards the breaking of this seal.

Apart from the famous 'lease-hold' of rectal dependency on which Lou Andreas-Salomé took a personal stand, they have generally kept to metaphors whose pitch of idealism indicates nothing deserving preference over what the first comer might offer us by way of less intentional poetry.

A congress on feminine sexuality is not going to hold over us the threat of the fate of Tiresias.

VI   The imaginary complex and questions of development

If it is the case that this state of things betrays a scientific impasse in our way of approaching the real, still the least one might expect of psychoanalysts, gathered at a congress, is that they bear in mind that their method was born precisely from a similar impasse.

If in this instance symbols have a purely imaginary hold, it is probably because the images are already subject to an unconscious symbolism, in other words to a complex – an apt moment to remind ourselves that images and symbols *for* the woman cannot be isolated from images and symbols *of* the woman.

It is representation (*Vorstellung* in the sense in which Freud uses the term to signal something repressed), the representation of feminine sexuality, whether repressed or not, which conditions how it comes into play, and it is the displaced offshoots of this representation (in which the therapist's doctrine can find itself implicated) which decide the outcome of its tendencies, however naturally roughed out one may take such tendencies to be.

Remember that Jones, in his lecture to the Viennese society which seems to have scorched the earth for any contribution since, already came up with nothing other than a pure and simple rallying to Kleinian concepts in the perfect crudity with which their author presents them: by which I mean Melanie Klein's persistent failure to acknowledge that the Oedipal fantasies which she locates in the maternal body originate from the reality presupposed by the Name of the Father.

When one thinks that this is all Jones manages to produce out of his grand design to resolve Freud's paradox, which sets up the woman in primary ignorance of her sex (although this is at least tempered by the informed admission of our ignorance) – a design which is so inspired in Jones by his prejudice for dominance by the natural that he is happy to sanction it with a quotation from Genesis – then it is none too clear what has been gained.

For in so far as it is a question of the wrong done to the female sex (is woman 'born or made' Jones cries) by the equivocal function of the phallic phase in the two sexes, then femininity does not seem to be made any more specific by the even more equivocal function which the phallus acquires when it is pushed right back to oral aggression.

So much fuss will not have been in vain if it allows us to play the following questions on the lyre of development, since that is the tune.

1. Is the bad object, which is extracted by a fantastic phallophagia from the breast of the maternal body, a paternal attribute?
2. When this object is raised to the status of a good object, which is desired as a more controllable (sic) and more satisfying nipple, (more satisfying in what?), then we have to ask: is this object taken from the same third party? For we cannot simply parade the notion of the combined parent, without knowing whether it is as image or symbol that this hybrid is constituted.
3. How does the clitoris, which, however autistic one would have it, none the less imposes itself in the real, come to be compared with the preceding fantasies?

If it independently places the sex of the little girl under the sign of an organic minus-value, then the way that its fantasies take on an aspect of endless reduplication renders highly suspect the 'legendary' fable of how these fantasies arise.

If the clitoris (it too) is combined with the bad as it is with the good object, then a theory is needed of how the phallus is assigned the function of equivalence in the emergence of all objects of desire, for which mention of its 'partial' character is not enough.
4. At all events, we arrive at the question of structure, which was introduced by Freud's approach: which means that the relation of privation or lack-in-being symbolised by the phallus, is established by derivation from the lack-in-having engendered by any particular or global frustration of demand. It is on the basis of this substitution, which in the last analysis the clitoris puts in its place before succumbing to the competition, that the field of desire precipitates its new objects (with the child to come at the fore), as it picks up the sexual metaphor into which all other needs had already entered.

This remark assigns to questions on development their limit by demanding their subordination to a fundamental synchrony.

VII Mistakes and prejudices

At this point we should also query whether phallic mediation
drains off the whole force of the drives in the woman, and
notably the whole current of the maternal instinct. Perhaps we
should also state here that the fact that everything that can be
analysed is sexual does not entail that everything sexual is
accessible to analysis.

1. As far as the supposed ignorance of the vagina is concerned,
while on the one hand it is difficult not to attribute to repression
its frequent persistence beyond the point of credibility, yet the
fact remains that, apart from certain case-studies (Josine Müller),
which we will disregard precisely because of the traumatic
character of their evidence, those who hold to the 'normal'
knowledge of the vagina are reduced to founding it on the
primacy of a downwards displacement of the experiences of the
mouth, that is, to a considerable worsening of the disagreement
they claim to palliate.
2. The problem of feminine masochism comes next, already
signalled by this promotion of a partial drive (a drive which is
regressive in its condition, whether or not one classifies it as pregenital) to the rank of one axis of genital maturity.

   In point of fact such a classification cannot be taken merely as
the homonym for a passivity which in itself is already metaphorical, and its idealising function, which is the other side of its
regressive note, is made glaringly obvious by the fact that it has
remained unchallenged in the face of the accumulation (possibly
overstated in modern analytical genesis), of the castrating and
devouring, dislocating and astounding effects of feminine
activity.

   Even given what masochistic perversion owes to masculine
invention, is it safe to conclude that the masochism of the woman
is a fantasy of the desire of the man?
3. Either way, the claim that fantasies of breaking bodily
frontiers can be deduced from an organic constant, for which the
rupture of the ovular membrane would be the prototype, can be
denounced as irresponsible idiocy. Such a crude analogy reveals
only too well the distance from Freud's way of thinking in this
area when he elucidated the taboo of virginity.
4. For what we are touching on here is the particular force dis-

tinguishing *vaginismus* from neurotic symptoms, even where the two co-exist, which explains its responsiveness to the suggestive method, whose success in painless deliveries is notorious.

If it is the case that analysis has got to the point of swallowing back its own vomit by tolerating a confusion of anxiety and fear within its orbit, perhaps this is the occasion to distinguish between unconscious and prejudice in relation to the effects of the signifier.

And simultaneously to acknowledge that the analyst is as prone as anyone else to prejudice about sex, over and above that which is revealed to him, or to her, by the unconscious.

Have we remembered Freud's often repeated warning not to reduce the supplement of feminine over masculine to the complement of passive to active?

VIII   Frigidity and the subjective structure

1. However widespread frigidity may be – and it is virtually generic if one takes into account its transitory form – it pre-supposes the whole unconscious structure which determines neurosis, even if it appears outside the web of the symptoms. This accounts on the one hand for its inaccessibility to any somatic treatment, and, on the other hand, for the normal failure of the good offices of the most wished-for of partners.

Analysis alone mobilises it, at times incidentally, but always in a transference which cannot be contained by the infantilising dialectic of frustration, that is, of privation, but one which always brings symbolic castration into play. In which context it is worth recalling a basic principle.

2. A principle which can be simply stated: that castration cannot be deduced from development alone, since it presupposes the subjectivity of the Other as the place of its law. The otherness of sex is denatured by this alienation. Man here acts as the relay whereby the woman becomes this Other for herself as she is this Other for him.

It is in this sense that an unveiling of the Other involved in the transference can modify a defence which has been taken up symbolically.

By which I mean that, in this case, defence should first be con-ceived of in the dimension of masquerade which the presence of the Other releases in its sexual role.

If we start by taking this veiling affect as our reference for object positions, then we might get some idea of how to deflate the monstrous conceptualisation whose credit in analytic circles I challenged above. Perhaps all that this conceptualisation shows is how everything gets ascribed to the woman in so far as she represents, in the phallocentric dialectic, the absolute Other.

We must therefore go back to penis envy (*penisneid*), where we note that at two different moments and each time with a certainty untroubled by any recollection of the other occasion, Jones makes of it a perversion and then a phobia.

The two appraisals are equally false and dangerous. The second indicates the abolition of the function of structure in the face of that of development, a position into which analysis has progressively slipped – this as against Freud's emphasis on phobia as the keystone of neurosis. In the first, analysis heads off into the labyrinth where the study of perversions has been attempting, with the utmost dedication, to account for the function of the object.

At the last turn in this palace of mirages, one ends up at the *splitting* of the object, having missed in Freud's admirable unfinished paper on the *splitting* of the *ego*, the *fading* of the subject which accompanies it.

Perhaps it will be this end point which finally lifts the illusion from the *splitting* in which analysis has got stuck by making good and bad into attributes of the object.

Inasmuch as the position of the sexes does differ in relation to the object, it is by all the distance which separates the fetishistic from the erotomanic form of love. We should find this standing out in the most common experience.

3. If we start with the man so as to measure the reciprocal position of the sexes, it is clear that the 'phallus-girls' of Fenichel's admirable if tentative equation, proliferate on a Venusberg way beyond the 'You are my wife' through which the man constitutes his partner, which confirms that what surfaces in the unconscious of the subject is the desire of the Other, that is, the phallus desired by the Mother.

This opens up the question of whether the real penis, in that it actually belongs to her sexual partner, commits the woman to an attachment without duplicity, granted the resolving of her incestuous desire whose course would in this argument be seen as natural. Taking this problem as settled, it can be posed the other way round.

4. Indeed, why not acknowledge that if there is no virility which castration does not consecrate, then for the woman it is a castrated lover or a dead man (or even both at the same time) who hides behind the veil where he calls on her adoration from that same place beyond the maternal *imago* which sent out the threat of a castration not really concerning her.

From then on, it is through this ideal incubus that a receptivity of embrace has to be transposed into the sensitivity of holding the penis.

It is this which is blocked by any imaginary identification on the part of the woman (in her stature as the object proffered to desire) with the phallic standard which upholds the fantasy.

In the position of either-or where the subject finds herself caught between a pure absence and a pure sensitivity, it is not surprising that the narcissism of desire immediately latches on to the narcissism of the *ego* which is its prototype. Analysis accustoms us to recognising that insignificant beings should be inhabited by so subtle a dialectic, which can also be explained by the fact that the least of the *ego's* failings is its banality.

5. The figure of Christ, which in this light conjures up others more ancient, can be seen here in a more widespread capacity than that which is called for by the religious allegiance of the subject. And it is worth noting that the unveiling of the most hidden signifier of the Mysteries was reserved to women.

At a more mundane level, one can thus account for:

(a) the fact that the duplicity of the subject is masked in the woman, all the more so in that the servitude of the spouse makes her particularly apt to represent the victim of castration;
(b) the true motive for the particular character of the demand for the fidelity of the Other on the part of the woman;
(c) the fact that it is easier for her to justify this demand by making the case of her own fidelity.

6. This outline of the problem of frigidity is sketched out in terms which can accommodate without difficulty the classical instances of analysis. Its broad outlines are intended to help avoid the pitfall which is progressively distorting the true nature of analytic works, as they come more and more to resemble a makeshift

bicycle, put together by a savage who had never seen one, out of components taken from models so historically remote as to have no correspondence to the original. Not that this prevents their being put to double use.

The least we can ask is that some elegance should brighten up the trophies thus obtained.

IX   Feminine homosexuality and ideal love

The study of the framework of perversions in the woman opens up a different bias.

1. Since it has been effectively demonstrated that the imaginary motive for most male perversions is the desire to preserve the phallus which involved the subject in the mother, then the absence in women of fetishism, which represents the virtually manifest case of this desire, leads us to suspect that this desire has a different fate in the perversions which she presents.

For to assume that the woman herself takes on the role of fetish, only raises the question of the difference of her position in relation to desire and to the object.

In the inaugural lecture of his series on the early development of feminine sexuality, Jones starts with his unusual experience of homosexuality in the woman, taking a line which he might have done better to sustain. He makes the desire of the subject branch off in the choice imposed on her between the incestuous object, in this case the father, and her own sex. The resulting clarification would be greater if it did not stop short at the too convenient prop of identification.

A better equipped observation would surely bring out that what is involved is more a taking up of the object: what might be called a challenge taken up. Freud's chief case, inexhaustible as always, makes it clear that this challenge is set off by a demand for love thwarted in the real and that it stops at nothing short of taking on the airs of a courtly love.

In that such a love prides itself more than any other on being the love which gives what it does not have, so it is precisely in this that the homosexual woman excels in relation to what is lacking to her.

Strictly speaking, it is not the incestuous object that the latter chooses at the price of her own sex; what she will not accept is that this object only assumes its sex at the price of castration.

Not that this means that she gives up on her own sex for all that: quite the contrary, in all forms of feminine homosexuality, including those which are unconscious, it is towards femininity that the supreme interest is borne, and Jones clearly detected here the link between the fantasy of the man as invisible witness and the care which the subject shows for the enjoyment of her partner.

2. We still have to take up the naturalness with which such women appeal to their quality of being men, as opposed to the delirious style of the transexual male.

Perhaps what this reveals is the path leading from feminine sexuality to desire itself.

Far from its being the case that the passivity of the act corresponds to this desire, feminine sexuality appears as the effort of a *jouissance* wrapped in its own contiguity (for which all circumcision might represent the symbolic rupture) to be *realised in the envy* of desire, which castration releases in the male by giving him its signifier in the phallus.

Could it be this privileging of the signifier that Freud is getting at when he suggests that there is perhaps only one libido and that it is marked with the male sign? Should some chemical configuration confirm this further, why not see this as the exalting conjunction of the molecular dissymetry employed by the living construction, with the lack concerted in the subject through language, so that the holders of desire and the claimants of sex (the partiality of the term being still the same here) work against each other as rivals?

X   Feminine sexuality and society

A number of questions remain concerning the social incidences of feminine sexuality.

1. Why is the analytic myth found wanting on the prohibition of incest between the father and daughter?

2. How should we situate the social effects of feminine homosexuality in relation to those which Freud attributed to masculine homosexuality, on the basis of assumptions remote from the

allegory to which they have since been reduced: that is, a sort of entropy tending towards communal degradation?

Without going so far as to set against this the antisocial effects to which Catharism, together with the love which it inspired, owed its disappearance, surely the more accessible movement of the *Précieuses*[1] shows the eros of feminine homosexuality as conveying the opposite of social entropy?

3. Finally, why does the social instance of the woman remain transcendant to the order of the contract propagated by work? And in particular, is it an effect of this that the status of marriage is holding out in the decline of paternalism?

All these are questions which cannot be reduced to a field regulated by needs.

Written two years before the Congress.

Note

1. *Les Précieuses*: a social and literary circle of ladies which centred around the Hotel Rambouillet in seventeenth-century Paris; they were renowned for their culture and for the refinement of their use of language (tr.).

CHAPTER FOUR
The Phallic Phase and the Subjective Import of the Castration Complex

Published in 1968, 'The Phallic Phase and the Subjective Import of the Castration Complex' is the first article written not by Lacan himself, but by a member of his school, which we include in this collection. It appeared in the first issue of Scilicet, *the journal of the* école freudienne. *This was the school of psychoanalysis founded by Lacan in 1964, following the unsuccessful attempt by the* Société française de psychanalyse *to affiliate to the* International Psychoanalytic Association. *The Society divided into those willing to recognise the condition laid down by the International (the exclusion of Lacan from the training programme) who founded the* Association psychanalytique de France, *and those who regrouped around Lacan.*

The first issue of Scilicet *appeared four years later. Apart from contributions by Lacan, the articles in the journal were unsigned. This article, which emerged out of a group project, was the first of the unsigned contributions. A list of contributors appeared at the end of the second issue.*

The article relates closely to Lacan's Seminar XI – the seminar he was giving at the time of the founding of the new school (Lacan, 1964) – from which it takes a number of its concepts. It is important for the extensive critical reassessment which it provides of the earlier Freud-Jones debate. While it recognises the limits of Freud's theses on the Oedipus complex and femininity, and the strength of many of Jones's clinical observations, it none the less argues that Jones's rejection of the concept of castration, and his reading of the phallic phase for both the boy and the girl child, commit him to a pre-psychoanalytic theory of the subject.

In this article, Lacan's theory of the subject's division in language is extended to include the field of the drive in its relation to the object, and the place of the subject in the cycle of sexed reproduction. At each of these levels, it is the difficulty of the subject's relationship to sexuality which is constantly at stake.

This article argues that it is the very inadequacy of Freud's account of femininity which enables us to focus that difficulty for the woman. Rather than reinstate feminine sexuality, in the way that Jones himself tried to do, it underscores the impossibility of the woman's position – whether as the object of sexual 'commerce', or else as a question or enigma which comes to embody the difficulty inherent within sexuality itself.

'The Phallic Phase and the Subjective Import of the Castration Complex' was published in Scilicet *(Lacan, 1968–76), I, 1968, pp. 61–84.*

The project of the present paper took shape during a reading, jointly undertaken by a working group, of a series of texts by Freud relating to the Oedipus complex, together with the texts published by Jones at the same period. It seemed to me that it might be of interest to take up these texts again, firstly because they bear on a crucial point of analytic theory, but above all in so far as the distance marked out between Freud and Jones testifies to an essential dimension of psychoanalytic experience. This is a dimension which Freud keeps to throughout his formulations on the castration complex and its repercussions for the feminine Oedipus complex, but one which Jones comes more and more deeply to evade.

Not that this is immediately apparent: at first glance, Jones appears more nuanced, more attentive to the evidence of analytic experience concerning the differences in the boy's and girl's approach to the Oedipus complex. And yet today, on the whole, the controversy has been settled, with Jones placed on the side of that reduction of experience which tends to turn analysis into a psychology of the *ego* and of adaptation to reality. Freud's pronouncements are still, however, in need of examination, so that we can try to grasp what he is getting at, in theses he adhered to with unswerving rigour over the years, and whose paradoxical character or seeming deadlock sparked off the great debate on the phallic phase and feminine sexuality which lasted from 1923 until 1935.

From among these contributions, whose continuing value for us lies in their having been pitted against Freud's original teaching, we will restrict ourselves here to the works of Jones (Jones 1927, 1933, 1935), precisely because of their bulk, the degree of theoretical elaboration which they demonstrate and the sharpness of the critical positions they take up with regard to Freud;

besides, Jones gives a full account of publications whose intention coincided with his own, in particular those of Melanie Klein and Karen Horney.

I

I will start with a very brief summary of the Freudian argument, bringing out above all those theses which were the object of Jones's criticisms.

The 1915 edition of the *Three Essays* left us with the assertion that infantile sexuality culminated in heterosexual object choice, without, however, the partial drives having converged or been subordinated to the primacy of the genital zone. In his article of 1923, Freud corrects this view by recognising that infantile sexuality 'at the height of its course of development',[1] reaches a true 'genital organisation', which none the less differs from the adult organisation in that 'for both sexes, only one genital, namely the male one, comes into account. What is present, therefore, is not a primacy of the genitals, but a primacy of the *phallus*.' On the basis of this assertion of a phallic phase (the term appears in 1924) common to the two sexes, Freud is able to give his well-known description of how the Oedipus complex in the boy is brought to an end by the crucial experience of seeing the female genitals; the threats against masturbation made earlier by the mother have a deferred effect. From then on, acceptance of the possibility of castration puts an end to two possible types of satisfaction (active or passive) linked to the Oedipus complex, as narcissistic interest in the penis gets the better of libidinal investment in parental objects. Phallic organisation breaks down on the threat of castration. But at the same moment the Oedipus complex is not only repressed, it is literally destroyed, and object cathexes are abandoned and replaced by identification (in particular with the father: the formation of the super-ego). We can note, therefore, that in these texts the phallic phase is introduced as essential for situating what is at stake in the ending of the Oedipus complex, since it is this phase which allows for the introduction of the key-function of castration.

In the case of the girl, the article of 1924 asserts the existence of a phallic phase and a castration complex, at the same time as mentioning that 'our material – for some incomprehensible reason – becomes far more obscure and full of gaps'. It is in fact in the two later articles of 1925 and 1931 that Freud sets out his views on the feminine Oedipus complex before his final account in the *New Introductory Lectures* in 1933. He starts with a new factor of his experience; a discovery as astounding as the discovery of the Cretan civilisation behind the civilisation of Greece – that is, the emergence of a long pre-Oedipal history in the girl: the Oedipal attachment to the father had been preceded by an extensive phase of attachment to the mother, not differing essentially from that which characterises the early years of the boy. This last point had already been made in the *Three Essays*, that, give or take a few shades of difference, the oral and anal phases are identical in the two sexes, but Freud now states that the same goes for the phallic phase – the clitoris plays a role homologous to that of the penis for the boy. Thus we begin to get the outlines of the double task awaiting the girl in the constitution of a normal Oedipal attitude: a change of her erotogenic zone and a change of her love-object.

But what are the motives which lead the girl to turn away from her mother? Freud tells us that they are numerous, obscure and surprising, and their very multiplicity suggests that the essential is missed. Yet it is the phallic phase which provides the guiding thread, precisely through its terminal point: the sight of the penis. Freud stresses the immediacy of its effect on the girl in contrast to the boy's long hesitation in admitting the reality of the woman's lack of penis. 'She makes her judgement and her decision in a flash. She has seen it and knows that she is without it and wants to have it' (XIX, 1925, p. 252). Then, latching on to this penis envy, comes the central reproach against the mother for not having given her one. From then on 'the girl slips – along the line of a symbolic equation, one might say – from the penis to a baby. Her Oedipus complex culminates in a desire, which is long retained, to receive a baby from her father as a gift' (XIV, 1924, pp. 178–9).

Such a rapid presentation inevitably slides over many points requiring detailed scrutiny; we will come back to some of them. For the moment what should be stressed is that the turning away from the mother represents more than 'a simple change of object' (XXII, 1933, p. 121), since it is accompanied by a reversal of love into hatred or resentment; hatred for the mother is, therefore, not to be understood in terms of Oedipal rivalry, but as the inheritance of this prehistory which, although it also covers that of the boy, retroactively takes on a different meaning after the castration complex. Freud, therefore, points to an essential assymmetry between the boy and the girl: 'It is only in the male child that we find the fateful combination of love for the one parent and simultaneous hatred for the other' (XXI, 1931, p. 229) – but, Freud states, we had long given up the hope of a perfect parallelism. If, at the end of the phallic phase 'in boys the Oedipus complex is destroyed by the castration complex, in girls it is made possible and led up to by the castration complex' (XIX, 1925, p. 256). This has the further result that for the girl 'the fear of castration being thus excluded, a powerful motive also drops out for the setting up of a super-ego' (XIX, 1924, p. 178); the Oedipus complex 'is all too often not surmounted by the female at all' (XXI, 1931, p. 230), whence also the absence of the cultural effects of its dissolution.

II

Thus, on the question of the ending of the Oedipus complex in the girl child, we arrive at a Freudian position which is certainly open to question and whose summary nature seems to have played its part in unleashing the great debate on the signification of the phallic phase in the girl.

For it was this issue that was later brought to the fore by a certain number of women analysts, in works which still hold the interest of having confronted the paradox which Freud opened up with the question of the phallus. From 1924 to 1932, the articles of Karen Horney (first to enter the lists), Melanie Klein, Josine Müller, Jeanne Lampl-de Groot and Ruth Mack Brunswick followed on each other – to cite only those contributions on which Jones (for the first three) and Freud (for the rest) came to rely in their quarrel.[2]

Let us start with a brief discussion of Jones's first article. Right from the beginning the standard is raised: 'Men analysts have been led to adopt an unduly phallo-centric view . . . the importance of the female organs being correspondingly underestimated.' We would already question whether it is legitimate to approach the problem of theoretical divergencies between analysts, on the basis of the interest or respect possibly motivating them in relation to any one 'organ'.

Jones starts with a critical reassessment of the psychoanalytic concept of castration, which he sees as obfuscating the issues by apparently referring to the idea of a 'total extinction of sexuality', an idea which it only in fact covers, more or less, in the case of the man. Jones proposes to substitute for it the concept of aphanisis, defined as 'the total and permanent extinction of the capacity for sexual enjoyment'. This already allows him to go back on the asymmetry indicated by Freud. Thus, if we admit in effect that all privation gives rise to the threat of aphanisis, and that privation is therefore 'equivalent to castration' ['frustration' in Jones's text], then we will see that 'both sexes ultimately dread exactly the same thing'. What this means for the girl is the non-gratification of her feminine desires, except that 'for obvious physiological reasons, the female is much more dependent on her partner for her gratification than is the male on his'. Fear of aphanisis expresses itself in her case largely in terms of a fear of separation. Thus, passing through an oral and anal phase distinguished by the early feminine direction of her libidinal life, the little girl will temporarily experience an auto-erotic penis envy, in which Jones recognises a brief parallelism with masculine development, but it is 'the comparative unsatisfactoriness of this solution which automatically guides the child to seek for a better external penis' (note that this is how Jones claims to sum up Freud's thesis). For Jones, however, this penis envy is of course allo-erotic, that is, it belongs to a successful feminine position, a position which can be blocked by the anxiety potentially linked to feminine desires, which then leads to a regression to the preceding phallic phase. It is this last possibility which covers the essential of Freud's phallic phase, which Jones therefore designates as a 'secondary, defensive construction rather than a true developmental stage'.

Breaking here with chronological order, I will now examine some of the ways in which Jones goes on to specify his conception of the feminine Oedipus complex, basing myself on the text of 1935.

Jones accords especial weight to the study of that 'feminine prehistory' which Freud spoke of, since the theoretical divergencies concerning the later stages follow from the conceptual differences relating to this phase. According to the London school, the little girl does not have the virile attitude which Freud ascribes to her: from the outset she is feminine, '*receptive and acquisitive*'; her preoccupations centre on the inside of her body (and that of her mother); what she wishes for, is to incorporate the objects contained in the mother (milk, the penis conceived of as a more satisfying nipple, and finally the penis of her father, which the mother has incorporated according to the fellatio theory of coitus). But for two reasons the sadism directed towards the mother's body is more anxiety ridden for her than for the boy. On the one hand, her anxiety relates essentially to the inside of her body and there is no external point of reference for narcissistic reassurance other than the clitoris; on the other hand, the girl's sexual rivalry is directed towards the very person on whom she depends for all her needs; the girl's sadism cannot therefore be externalised and is turned inwards far more on her than on the boy – whence her drawn-out dependency on the mother and the 'especially inexorable repression' which Freud says later characterises this relationship. There is, therefore, an early vaginal position, but one which often cannot be expressed, notably on account of the fact that the vagina is not inhabited at that stage by any physiological function and is 'relatively inaccessible', meaning that it cannot be used by the little girl as a reality or libidinal reassurance.

For Jones, the phallic phase described by Freud is indeed partly linked to 'the simple auto-erotic envy' of a penis, but the wish to have a penis in the place of a clitoris in fact derives from essentially defensive secondary motives, linked to the anxiety produced by the urethral sadism which dominates this period. The best way of reassuring oneself against this sadism would be to carry it into effect and so experience that it is not mortal, which is what the boy does, reassuring himself when he sees that his penis remains intact. For, while it may be a weapon for attacking the mother, the penis also, and above all, serves restitutive ends and, in the last analysis, what the girl essentially envies is this effective form of defence which it places at the disposal of the boy. Jones makes a distinction between this auto-erotic wish on the part of the girl to possess a penis of her own and 'a primary natural wish for a penis' which should be seen not as a masculine striving but as 'the normal feminine desire to incorporate a man's penis inside her body – first of all by an oral route, later by a vaginal one'.

The dissolution of the phallic phase is, therefore, nothing other than the surfacing of a previously repressed femininity, and from here Jones can go on to propose a different connection between penis envy and hostility towards the mother. For Freud, the disappointed little girl 'wisely resigns herself to seeking other sources of pleasure that will console her' (here Jones scarcely conceals his irony). But if the phallic phase is merely a 'phallic position', an 'emotional attitude rather than a stage in libidinal development', then the reasons for its dissolution do not differ as such from those leading to a gradual disappearance of an infantile phobia in proportion to an increasing 'adaptation to reality'. In the case of the girl's phallic phase, the defensive fantasy of the penis is relinquished because it is recognised as a fantasy and hence as incapable of providing the reassurance of external reality. The ego has strengthened, anxiety has diminished, and the little girl is now capable of recognising in her mother a real person to whom she is tied by affection. Finally, the stage of part-object love has been outgrown and the little girl is now interested in her father 'as a whole' [English in the original]. Resentment against the mother thus corresponds to the Oedipal rivalry which has long been present, but which can at last express itself.

Thus for Jones, femininity does not arise as it does for Freud from an 'external experience' (the sight of the penis), any more than the phallic phase is 'a natural reaction to an unfortunate anatomical fact'; it 'develops progressively from the promptings of an instinctual constitution'; woman is not this '*homme manqué*, a permanently disappointed creature, struggling to console herself with secondary substitutes alien to her true nature'. Is woman 'born or made' Jones finally exclaims, echoing the conclusion of his 1933 article: 'In the beginning . . . male and female created He them.'

We will start by questioning this innate and natural character which Jones confers on both femininity and masculinity when he postulates their direct insertion into biological sexual bipolarity, for this is ultimately what governs the whole of his disagreement with Freud. One might wonder how this could be anything other than a prejudice of a naturalist order, which nothing in our practice can truly sustain. For it is obvious that analytic experience has no point of contact, and makes no direct link with a bipolarity of the sexes such as would be given in nature. We need only to reflect that, for as long as it has existed, psychoanalysis has made no contribution to the development of biological knowledge on sexuality, any more than it has drawn from it the least sustenance. For example, any difficulties experienced by the individual in assuming his or her own sex, bear no direct relation to the biological facts of what is called intersexuality. All the evidence goes to show that analysis approaches the question from a completely different, and strictly subjective, angle, what we could call the angle of a subjective declaration of sex. On this point, therefore, Jones's position is outside what specifies the analytic field, and the most one could do would be to refer it back to biology for corroboration. But if his point of view strikes us as more naturalistic than biologistic, it is in so far as biology itself seems to have progressed only by moving away from such a crude assertion of sexual bipolarity, by dividing it up, for example, into heterogeneous levels (chromosomes, hormonal layers, primary and secondary sexual characteristics), leaving room for some discontinuities and for some questioning of what might be involved in any strict demarcation of male and female.

Again, what arguments from within analytic experience is he able to adduce in support of his thesis? None other, finally, than the identification of drives with a passive aim, and that is precisely where we can pinpoint his divergence from Freud.

For we know how Freud insisted on the hiatus he saw as separating the contrast masculine–feminine from the contrast activity–passivity; I am referring to three texts by Freud (Freud, VII, 1905, XIV, 1915, XXI, 1931) which are, incidentally, well known, and which clearly state that the polarity activity–passivity is the only one with any meaning at the level of the theory of the drives; the coalescence of this polarity with the polarity masculine–feminine 'meets us as a biological fact; but it is by no means so invariably complete and exclusive as we are inclined to assume' (XIV, 1915, p. 134). In actual fact the question of this coalescence is left entirely open by Freud and in any case, the opposition masculine–feminine can only come into consideration at the end of the Oedipus complex, which is enough to situate it in an entirely different register from the biological. Finally, and above all, Freud ends up by stating that there is nothing corresponding to the terms masculine and feminine which can be directly grasped as such in our experience.

Alongside this, Freud maintains that there exists 'a single libido, which, it is true, has both active and passive aims (that is, modes of satisfaction)' (XXI, 1931, p. 240) – 'libido is invariably and necessarily of a masculine nature, whether it occurs in men or in women and irrespectively of whether its object is a man or a woman' (VII, 1905, p. 219). What we are given to understand by this is that the dialectic of the partial drives is governed by the phallic instance for both sexes, precisely because this dialectic is of a different order from that of biological sexual difference. The Freudian approach consists of trying to see how these two heterogeneous registers intersect, that is to say, how biological difference comes to interact with the play of the drives. It is a question of knowing not 'what a woman is' but 'how a woman develops out of a child with a bisexual disposition' – and here, Freud adds, 'the constitution will not adapt itself to its function without a struggle'. From this point, everything that can be grasped in analytic experience will be articulated in terms of 'the psychical consequences of the anatomical distinction between the sexes', a title which in itself indicates the distance separating the real of sexual difference from its subsequent reverberations as impasses in the subjectivisation of sex.

It is worth bringing out these themes more clearly in relation to what Freud has to say about the evolution of the girl. First of all, when he tackles the question of what finally leads the little girl to relinquish the maternal object and turn towards the father, we see him so keen to avoid any recourse to a pre-given libidinal femininity that he centres the whole of his interrogation on the contrast activity–passivity in relation to the drives (a contrast so far from being biological in nature that it is supported entirely by grammatical oppositions). This same contrast is explicitly referred to the death drive, in the form of the little girl's tendency to repeat actively on her dolls what she has undergone passively in relation to her mother (a perfect example of the extent to which Jones misinterprets this text when he reproaches Freud for failing to recognise in this that the little girl derives a libidinal satisfaction of a feminine type from this game). At this stage there is no question of femininity precisely in so far as the dialectic of the drives stops, on the level of the infantile genital organisation, at an opposition which can only be 'having a male genital and being castrated' (XIX, 1923, p. 145). Jones can claim to be refining on Freud's argument by suggesting that in the case of the girl, the opposition should be posed as possessing the clitoris or not, but he merely demonstrates his failure to distinguish between organ and symbol. It is, however, this symbolic reference which Freud so heavily underlines when he describes the Oedipus complex as 'a phenomenon which is determined and laid down by heredity and which is bound to pass away according to programme when the next pre-ordained phase of development sets in' (XIX, 1924, p. 174). What could this programme be, other than that peculiar and yet predetermined ordering of the signifying chain which pre-exists the subject, and in which the phallic symbol finds its place and its function? The symbolic equivalence penis = baby operates at this level, and it is amusing to see Jones flattering himself that his mode of theorisation has given to this equivalence a 'more natural' foundation.

Finally, if Freud characterises the pre-Oedipal attitude of the girl as virile, it is, therefore, on the one hand in order to acknowledge the predominance in her of drives with an active aim (the Oedipal period will substitute a 'wave of passivity' for these drives without giving the slightest access to what might be the essence of the feminine); and on the other hand, in order to point out that the girl is subject on the same count as the boy to the phallic dialectic, which is alone capable of introducing the subject to the ideals of his or her sex.

Jones is, therefore, operating a kind of short circuit when he places masculinity and femininity in an unmediated relationship to anatomical difference, a relationship of which they have no knowledge. They take on their meaning only in a completely other register, that is, the symbolic register in so far as it is within this register that the ego ideal is determined. And it is precisely this privileged moment of access to the symbolic register that Freud is pointing to in the castration complex. Which is exactly why, by taking the question as settled from the start, Jones can only miss and profoundly mis-recognise the dimension of castration. We can take as proof of this the sliding in his terminology from anxiety to fear of castration, or better still, his promotion of the strange concept of aphanisis.

The context and way in which Jones uses this concept effectively rule out its having any other meaning than that of a disappearance of desire, fear of which would be at the centre of what Freud identifies as castration anxiety. But could such a fear really constitute that pivotal point, that radical term of our experience which Jones intends by it? How can we conceive of a disappearance of desire – a desire which Freud tells us is indestructible – other than as a repression? And if this is the case, then can we attribute to the subject a fear or repression at the very moment when it is operating? Furthermore, anxiety has nothing to do with disappearance of desire: it is only too obvious that it refers to the object concealed behind it, in so far as the means of locating what it is that the Other desires, to use the precise terms, can be found wanting. Doubtless aphanisis of desire corresponds to a recognisable stage in the clinical treatment of neurosis: but this should not stop us from seeing that the neurotic, far from fearing it, seeks refuge in it, and pretends to give up his or her desire in order to safeguard that which is more precious than desire itself – its symbol, the phallus. Which means that by entering into the discourse on aphanisis, the analyst becomes equally complicit in the attempt to avoid what is unbearable in the castration complex. Hence it is that the concept of aphanisis, put forward in 1927 in order to get beyond the partiality of the Freudian concept and to guarantee at all costs the symmetry of the complex in both sexes, then disappears from the later writings, while the concept of castration is progressively watered down into an opaque reference to primitive non-gratification, and analytic theory works more and more to close off the fissures in which the implications of this concept should properly be located.

What follows is nothing other than the consequences of this major elision, consequences whose scope I will bring out merely so as to convey what the Freudian way of posing the problem enables us to avoid. First, an overriding reference to the organ and the biological, and to a satisfaction indistinguishable from that of a need (whereas when Freud gave exemplary status to the enigma of sexual satisfaction, he simultaneously introduced the dimensions of repetition and the lost object); secondly, a telescoping of the distinct registers of privation, frustration and castration in favour of an imaginary dialectic centred on the couple frustration–gratification; and finally, a foregrounding of the criterion of adaptation to reality in which the very issue in dispute is taken for granted – namely, the moment of castration, as the moment which should be located as the very instigation of the subject in the confrontation with the real of sexual difference. Thus we see Jones conjuring up the figure of the 'real mother', with nothing to distinguish her from the mirror games which preceded her arrival. From the 'real' object, we slide again onto the 'whole' object, without any theorisation of this outgrowing of the part-object, which, if we go by the Freudian estimation, is, to say the least, open to question.

In this context, the phallic phase could in no sense be given the central function which Freud assigns to it in the structuring of the subject. In the case of the girl, it is literally for Jones a contradiction in terms which can no longer be anything other than a defensive formation, inevitable in the sense that infantile neurosis might be inevitable. And in 1935 it is presented by Jones as having a phobic structure (when he had assimilated it to a perversion in 1932, as we will see, and had reproached Freud as early as 1927 for conceiving of the masculine phallic phase in terms of a phobia).

III

Challenged by Freud (Freud, XXI, 1931), Jones replies in 1932 with his major article on the phallic phase. He opens it by proposing to divide the phallic phase into a proto-phallic phase and a deutero-phallic phase. It is in fact easy to see why this latter phase in the girl could only be conceived of by Jones as being in the order of a second stage, given that he sees it as so contrary to the connaturality linking her to her biological sex. But the logic of his position leads him to throw the phallic phase of the boy equally into question and to identify in it a 'defensive' function, thereby restoring the parallelism between the two sexes which is so dear to him. His procedure is, therefore, clear: first, he proposes the distinction in order to clarify the issues and to limit his disagreement with Freud to the deutero-phallic phase, but in the end it transpires that the term proto-phallic 'is unnecessary and can even be misleading'.

Here, very briefly then, is the conception Jones proposes for the masculine Oedipus complex. In accordance with Kleinian theorisation, the stress is laid on the importance of the oral drives and the sadism unleashed by their frustration. The latter leads the child to attribute to its mother a penis like its own, which 'is mainly a more satisfying and nourishing nipple', but because of ambivalence, it is transformed by projection into a threatening organ which has to be destroyed by oral incorporation. The ambivalence is intensified when, during the second year, the father's penis becomes involved in this associative series, and this regardless of the existence even of a real father (the concept of the 'combined parent'). Sadism makes an early link between the oral

and phallic registers, the boy's own penis coming into his fantasies as a weapon aimed at forging a path to the sources of oral
satisfaction concealed in the maternal body. But such an attitude
of appropriation on oral and then anal lines places the boy in a
feminine position by bringing him up against the paternal penis
'dwelling' in the mother's organ, at the same time as the vagina is
transformed by projection into a destructive cavity. Castration
anxiety is, therefore, firmly linked to the Oedipus complex, but
it is conceived of as resulting from the retaliation of the oral drive
whose object is the paternal penis. It then follows that what is at
stake cannot be the castration of the mother (which Jones sees as a
rationalisation), but the castration of the boy or of his father.

What repercussions does this account ascribe to the sight of the
female genital organ? This experience, Jones tells us, gives an
actuality to fear of castration 'by arousing the possibility that a
dangerous repressed wish may be gratified in reality'. Jones,
therefore, reduces this moment to the point of making it homologous to a reality test. In Freudian theory, however, the place of
reality-testing is carefully specified, that is, it is strictly immanent
to the dialectic of the pleasure and reality principles, which is to
say, that it operates within a purely egoic economy. In other
words, it is fundamentally inadequate for any understanding of
the object dealt with in analysis, in so far as this object is characterised as an object of desire and testifies to a different reality –
that of the drive which, erupting outside the field of narcissism,
has to be situated as a transgression in relation to the pleasure
principle. This is what makes for its profound affinity with the
symbolic register. The drive marks the subject's attempt to
realise itself in the field of the Other and to find in that field the
object which is eternally lacking. Satisfaction of the drive is
consequently open to question, so much so that one could argue
that the entire Freudian theory of the drives is designed to point
to our state of uncertainty on the function of satisfaction.
Remember that, as regards satisfaction of the drives, the object
can strictly be termed indifferent, and that in the case of sub-
limation, satisfaction is obtained even though the drive is
inhibited in relation to its aim. Which shows that the satisfaction
involved could not be that of a need, nor even that of a demand
such as can move in falsely to fill up the lack of desire, and that
when Freud elevated sexual satisfaction to such an exemplary
position, he was simultaneously underlining its limits and

impasses: 'we must reckon with the possibility that something in the nature of the sexual instinct itself is unfavourable to the realisation of complete satisfaction'(XI, 1912, pp. 188–9).

To say that the penis represents in the imaginary 'a more satisfying nipple', can, therefore, in no way help us to grasp the subjective import of the perception of the female genital organ. Rather it tends to elide what Freud so emphatically stressed as a confrontation with a lack, whose essential link with the function of representation as such he immediately underlined, and which, as something which can be designated in the real, necessarily refers to the dimension of the symbolic (since there is nothing missing in the real). It is in this symbolic register that the subject must be constituted before anything belonging to the order of desire can take on a structure for him. 'Sooner or later the child, who is so proud of his possession of a penis, has a view of the genital region of the little girl, and cannot help being convinced of the absence of a penis in a creature who is so like himself. With this, the loss of his own penis becomes imaginable' (XIX, 1924, pp. 175–6) – the context showing that it is around the retroactive effect of this experience that other losses of 'highly valued parts of the body' (breasts, faeces) will later be organised.

By stressing the import of this 'test of the desire of the Other' (MP, p. 83), Freud makes it clear that what is at issue for him throughout this moment of castration is the mode of representation of a lack from which the subject finds himself suspended in his relation to desire: whence the traumatic, unbearable character of this perception and of the profound fissure in which it establishes the subject.

Jones thinks he can give a better account than Freud's of the link between castration anxiety and 'dread of the vulva'. For him this link clearly presupposes the infantile sadistic theory of coitus and an early knowledge of the vagina: 'If there were no dangerous cavity to penetrate into there would be no fear of castration.' Obviously: since the natural function of the penis is penetration, we are bound to come across, early on, an '*impulse to penetrate*' [English in the original], and consequently, alongside it, the intuition of 'a penetrable cavity'. 'The proposition that the boy has no intuition of the sex difference is on logical grounds alone hard to hold.' To which all we can say is that such is Jones's fascination with the complementarity of the sexes that he makes a forced entry of their difference into a logic which, to say the least, does not accommodate it with quite the same ease.

It follows from this that for Jones the phallic phase of the boy is of course 'a neurotic compromise rather than a natural evolution in sexual development', this being already established in his eyes by the ignorance of the vagina and the wiping out of any impulse towards penetration during this phase. The phallic phase consists of a narcissistic reassurance serving to master 'deep anxieties from various sources'.

Certainly it is the case that such observations correspond to facts which can be discerned during the course of an analytic treatment, and there is no question of denying the accuracy of the clinical observations offered by Jones and the authors to whom he appeals; they are of indisputable value when related to certain definite structures or moments in the course of analytic treatment. But the same cannot be said of their theoretical interpretation. For example, Jones sets himself the enigma of why 'so many men feel unable to put something into a woman unless they have first got something out of her' or again 'why should imperfect access to the nipple give a boy the sense of imperfect possession of his own penis'. Without going into the details of what such a case might imply, I will say that it immediately touches on a basic feature, which must be brought out as the correct starting point for its elaboration – namely, that the sexual function is only assured precisely by the passage through the castration complex, castration indeed being first located in the mother, whose lack as desiring is what throws the child onto the law of the father. Instead of which, Jones interprets the clinical facts in terms of ambivalent oral drives centred on the penis of the father, and naturally for Jones it could only be a question of the paternal penis, since the mother has not got a 'real' penis. The basis for the lack to which castration introduces the subject is then referred back to the intervention of an even more archaic oral aggressivity. At the same time, the lack of symbolic reference makes it necessary to play on the dialectic real father–imaginary father, not that locating this in the earlier phases can in any way help to account for the place of the paternal function in the Oedipal structure.

It is along these lines that the phallic phase finally appears to Jones as a phallic perversion: 'The previous heterosexual allo-eroticism of the early phase is in the deutero-phallic one . . . largely transmuted into a substitutive homosexual auto-eroticism.' This in itself calls for a lengthy discussion. Let us note simply, that, if the perverse structure effectively stands in a determinate relation to the phallic phase, then Jones's formula is already problematic in that it is given as valid for both sexes. For Freud is careful to leave on one side the question of feminine perversion, with all its vast difficulty, by ascribing the very nucleus of perversion, that is, fetishism, to an accident of the masculine phallic phase. Furthermore, he bases this, not on any identificatory mechanism, but on the subjective effect of the sight of the female genital organ, in which he recognises that structural element which later leads him to the introduction of the *Ichspaltung* [the splitting of the ego].

Finally, one last difficulty in Jones's text on the masculine Oedipus complex. We are told that at all events the phallic phase could only constitute a temporary impasse leading off from the normal path of development. The young boy 'has later to retrace his steps in order to evolve, he has to claim again what he had renounced – his masculine impulses to reach the vagina'. One could find no better way of expressing just how far the castration complex has here lost its true meaning, which is to constitute the object as lost. But the whole point is that, for Jones, the object is in no sense lost: it is present and ready to saturate the needs of the subject, provided the latter manages to adapt to reality and to enter into what psychoanalytic theory has since celebrated under the name of genital love. Within such a conception of the all-satisfying relations of an organism to its *Umwelt*, one is bound to recognise that there is no place for the true dimension of castration, any more than for the Oedipus complex itself, as designating the enigma of an unattainable *jouissance*.

We should, therefore, be wary when we see Jones rejoice at being 'plus royaliste que le roi', and for reaching unitary formulas which seem to him to give a symmetrical account of the feminine and masculine positions regarding both the phallic phase and the Oedipus complex. For one has to allow that Jones has triumphed: he lets it be known that he has substituted for simplistic theories which try to bend experience to their *a priori* assumptions, a theory which is certainly more complicated, but one which can at least account for the insertion of the subject into his, or her, sexual nature.

Yet it is the uncertainty of this insertion that Freud is pointing to in the castration complex. As such it represents a theoretical impasse, because any theory tends as if by its very nature to cover over this radical fissure, and a subjective impasse, because the subject is called on to face in it the lack through which he is constituted. This is the uncomfortable point Freud has left us at by designating the castration complex as the bedrock of his experience. That Jones was able for a time to veil over the question would seem to be indicated by the surprising extinction of the debate after his last communication of 1935, not that we cannot sense in that article the trace of his own stupefaction, as well as the ambiguous function of the amnesia which it produced.

IV

The gap between Jones and Freud is, therefore, a perfect demonstration of the extent to which there is one dimension of experience which constantly runs the risk of falling from the primacy Freud assigns to it. For, it was a necessity intrinsic to the symbolic order, one which we have learnt from Lacan to read as the effect of the subject's dependency on the signifier, that led Freud to designate the very instigation of the subject by the name of castration. This is what dictates that we should try to grasp that articulation again now, since it alone can account for Freudian 'phallocentrism' and for the paradox of the castration complex, as a process of cancellation involving the very organ which thereby receives its proper place in the subjective economy.

Let us, therefore, start with lack, inscribed at the roots of the structure in so far as the subject is constituted in a dependency on the speech of the Other. From this point on, the particularity of his need can only be abolished in demand, a demand which can never be satisfied, since it is always the demand for something else. This is also why the particularity of need has to resurface in the desire which develops on the edge of demand. Now, the very meaning of the Oedipus complex is to introduce the subject to the dimension of desire by putting an end to an economy centred on demand, and it is this that confers its privileged value on the sight of the female genitals, which was given by Freud the status of a crucial experience: in this moment the lack in the Other serves the function of turning away the subject which is essential to the constitution of the Oedipal triangulation. But all he has to go on is that which supports the desire of the Other, that is, the phallic symbol whose role in the subjective economy is precisely to supplement the *signifiance* of the Other at the very point where it is found wanting. The price of the subject's access to the world of desire is that the real organ must be marked at the imaginary level with this bar, so that its symbol can take up its place as the signifier of this very point where the signifier is lacking. And when Freud gives the boy's narcissistic attachment to his penis as his motive for renouncing the mother, he is indicating how the imaginary function lends itself to such symbolisation. On the level of the narcissistic economy, investment in the penis cannot pass over into the specular image where it is replaced by an empty space, meaning that the penis has already been cancelled out at the imaginary level.

To be more specific, the lack inscribed in the signifying chain through which the Other, as the only possible site of truth, reveals that it holds no guarantee, is in terms of the dialectic of desire a lacking in *jouissance* of the Other. That there must somewhere be *jouisssance* of the Other is the only possible check on the endless circulating of significations – but this can only be ensured by a signifier, and this signifier is necessarily lacking. It is as his payment to this place that the subject is called upon to make the dedication of his castration – the negative mark bearing on the organ at the imaginary level (the lack of phallic image in the image desired) is positivised as phallic symbol, the signifier of desire. Hence the fact that, in so far as *jouissance* is auto-erotic, there is a limit or bar imposed on it. This is what is meant by saying that the Oedipus complex constitutes *jouissance* as forbidden by relying on paternal law, a dimension which has been increasingly evaded since Freud and one whose difficulty Jones merely displaces by referring the Oedipal triangulation back to the oral phase.

We can now see more clearly the basis for the privileging of the phallus, but also the disparity which anatomical difference introduces into the symbolic process and the reason for the difficulty which the theory has in producing an account of this process in the woman. It is certainly a major difficulty since it led Freud to uphold a position on the feminine Oedipus complex and its likely non-resolution (as opposed to the 'dissolution' of the masculine Oedipus complex), which could fairly be described as paradoxical – hence the heated note in 'feminist' arguments whose traces can be detected in this discussion.

But was the rush to rehabilitate the woman the best counter to Freud's argument, or does it not rather bear the marks of a retreat in the face of the very problem it seeks to address?

The first point to make is that by stating the universality of the process of castration as the unique path of access to desire and to sexual normativisation, Freud was doing no more than upholding the prevalence of the symbolic order in relation to any access to subjectivity. Of course, feminine destiny then became problematic, as Freud's failure to account for the girl's relation to the law at the end of the Oedipus complex clearly demonstrates. This difficulty is not, however, insoluble, if we push the categories Freud himself disengaged beyond the use he was able to make of them, and draw a distinction, as regards castration, between the symbolic principle (sacrifice or gift), the real organ (penis or clitoris) which it is the function of the phallus to symbolise, and the imaginary effects resulting from it which Freud showed as branching off into the two channels of the castration complex and penis envy. This is not the place to set against Jones another theory of what characterises the feminine position in this respect, and I will not go over here the structural features which Lacan has taught us to recognise in this position by means of these categories, except to note that they dispel any lingering shadows of an alleged inferiority of the 'being without a penis'.

But that still doesn't take the investigation Freud was pursuing as far as it can go. For if it is the case today that we can elaborate a conception of the feminine Oedipus complex which is coherent enough to follow Freud's teaching while also removing the difficulties that someone like Jones came up against, this does not mean, and this has to be said, that the feminine enigma has any the more ceased to engage us. To see this we need only consider all that remains unresolved on the question of feminine orgasm and frigidity. Thus we have yet to clarify the true meaning of what Freud sensed as a carrying over onto the woman of the difficulty inherent in sexuality, in so far as its subjective acquisition is problematic. Moreover, whatever can be stated about the constitution of the feminine position in the Oedipus complex or in the sexual 'relation' concerns only a second stage, one in which the rules governing a certain type of exchange based on a common value have already been established. It is at a more radical stage, constitutive of these very rules themselves, that Freud points to one last question by indicating that it is the woman who comes to act as their support. This is the question which challenges the subject from the place of the Other, in that the difference between the sexes introduces a non-representable instance which is found to coincide with the point of failing that the subject encounters in the signifying chain.

This formulation becomes clearer if we go back to the drive. Besides, it should be stressed that the above resumé of the structure in which desire occurs does not give a direct account of its essential link with sexuality, since it takes this as already given by designating the phallus as the signifier of desire.

The drives represent the cause of sexuality in the psychic; they do so only partially and yet they constitute the only link of sexuality to our experience.

Remember that it is in the context of the theory of the drives that, very early on in his work, Freud designates the object as radically lost. In a way scarcely compatible with Jones's enthroning of the 'whole' parent, Freud teaches us that it is at that moment of the oral drive when the child gains access to a complete representation of its mother as such, that the breast, as part-object, is constituted as lost – an irreducible feature of the object which, in the child's attempts at recovery, already points to the dimension of repetition which Freud later introduces with the death drive, in its essential connection to language.

This function of the part can, however, only be understood as resulting from the intersection of two distinct registers. First, from the point of view of the biological function supporting it, the drive only represents that function partly, or even partially, a fact of experience already demonstrated by the very topography of the erotogenic zones in limiting themselves to an edge.

But the basis for this lies in something belonging to the sexual function itself, whose presence in the living being, subordinated to it for his reproduction, stamps this being as mortal. If the drive represents the cause of sexuality, it can only do so by taking back onto itself this lack inscribed in the very fact of sexed reproduction. Secondly, from the point of view of the signifying chain, the subject, by being constituted in dependency on that chain, undergoes a loss. One part of himself is thrown up as the residue of his entry into the field of the Other – part-objects, or detachable parts of the body, whose structure is based on a feature of anatomical division due to its homology with signifying divisions. It is at the junction of these two registers that the subject, because he is subject to speech, pays the tribute of his pound of flesh to the Other. But the essential point to remember here is the link of the sexual drive to death, if we are to see that it is well and truly his own death that the subject comes to lay at the place where he encounters the lack of the Other.

This is the point of insertion of sexuality into the structure: the loss to which sexuality already testifies as a biological function comes to coincide with the lack inscribed in the signifying chain. What is, on the side of desire, the impossibility of adequately representing sexuality, is, on the side of the Other, lack of a signifier. There is only one libido, meaning that there is no psychic representative of the opposition masculine–feminine. The essence of castration and the link of sexuality to the unconscious both reside in this factor – that sexual difference is refused to knowledge [*savoir*], since it indicates the point where the subject of the unconscious subsists by being the subject of non-knowledge. It is from here that what cannot be spoken of sexual difference gets transposed into the question with which the Other, from the place of its lack, interrogates the subject on *jouissance*. What we still need to understand is in what sense it is the woman who comes to embody this question, at that point of obscurity where Freud set himself the query: 'What does a woman want?'

Let us, therefore, go back to the castration complex, inasmuch as its effect is to ensure the *signifiance* of the Other at the point where it is wanting. That the Other should thereby act as guarantee is the founding condition for any possibility of exchange, and what must be given up to this is the *jouissance* of the subject. The castration complex thus designates the passing of *jouissance* into the function of a value, and its profound adulteration in that process. Now, what happens is that this share, which is necessary to the setting up of a common value, is apportioned from male *jouissance*, precisely in so far as the function of detumescence lends itself to the symbolisation of a conceivable disappearance or wiping out of this residue of the subject (the part-object). The fact that this third term can seem to disappear for an instant is effectively the only thing which sustains the vanishing moment of satisfaction. But by becoming the place to which it is transferred, it is the woman who finds herself representing this phallic value. Thus, at the moment when sexual exchange, governed by the law of supply and demand, is initiated, the woman comes to figure as the object of *jouissance*. But what about her own *jouissance*? We can see now the reason why the Freudian inquiry stalled on this question, its relevance for challenging the very basis of the subject's relation to the Other, and also the blind alley the question necessarily leads to if one fails to see that the woman only becomes the support of this relation in a second stage, and at that level of fiction which is commonly labelled sexual commerce. In this the woman will play her part, but it is of course elsewhere that she upholds the question of her own *jouissance*.

This is the path traced out for us if we want to take into account the advance made by Freud. Certainly, the 'feminine mystery' can fairly be designated the alienation point of Freudian theory, provided one adds that it was Freud himself who identified it as such, and that, by taking it as far as his experience demanded, he has made it possible for us to glimpse its truth. By failing, on the other hand, to recognise it as alienation, Jones was driven to a naturalism which could only refer to the real of biological difference without being able to account for its effective repercussions for the subject other than by recourse to the imaginary register. This was not accidental since it is indeed through the mediation of demand that the sexual function enters into the circuit of desire. But the predominance of demand is precisely what characterises the neurotic in his dependency on the demand of the Other, as he flees from the point where his desire places his being in question.

This place of desire is exactly what requires that we uphold the different instances through which the biological sexual function is articulated in relation to the dimension of the signifier, and in which, simultaneously, the subject of the unconscious is founded. Basing myself on the teaching of Lacan, I have attempted to distinguish the separate registers in which this dialectic is played out and to situate their intersection in the concept of castration. It is, furthermore, the only way of accounting both for the place which analytic theory reserves to sexuality and the exclusive way it is dealt with in our *praxis*, that is, as entirely caught up in the retroactive function of symbolic determination, from which all subjective effects are governed.

Notes

1. I have followed the translation of Freud as given in the French text even where this varies slightly from the equivalent passage of The Standard Edition or in the articles by Ernest Jones (tr.).
2. Apart from the references given by Jones in the articles quoted, for biblio-graphical information, see Janine Chasseguet-Smirgel (1964 (1981)) – the introduction to this book gives a summary of the whole series of works. [See also complete bibliography at the end of translated texts (tr.)].

CHAPTER FIVE

Feminine Sexuality in Psychoanalytic Doctrine

'Feminine Sexuality in Psychoanalytic Doctrine' was published in 1975 in Scilicet, no. 5. It was later revised as the first chapter of Moustafa Safouan's La sexualité féminine dans la doctrine freudienne which appeared in Lacan's collection, le champ freudien at Editions du Seuil in 1976 (Safouan, 1976). Safouan was a member of the école freudienne who had been with Lacan since 1953. In 1980, when Lacan dissolved the school in response to what he saw as a compromise and dispersal of his work, Safouan made a direct commitment to what then became Lacan's Cause freudienne. In a further division in 1981, he left to join the Centre d'études et de recherches freudiennes.

This article formed part of a project to reconsider the main aspects of Freud's account of femininity in terms of the work of Lacan. It addresses not only Freud's theses, but also those of his opponents, and brings into its argument material from American research on female sexuality (Masters and Johnson) which has been equally important in recent feminist criticisms of Freud.

The article concentrates on the issue of phallicism in relation to the specific difficulties which Freud identified in the Oedipus complex of the girl child. The problem of the girl's relinquishment of her mother is examined through the very wording of the question which Freud himself failed to answer – 'What does the little girl want of her mother?' Safouan argues that behind that question we can discern the structure of desire, which he analyses, following Lacan, in terms of the divisions of the linguistic utterance itself.

It is the importance of this article that it recognises the problem of the girl's entry into the Oedipus complex, not as something to be resolved, but as an issue which demands a reformulation of the theory of the unconscious and sexuality in their relation to language.

'Feminine Sexuality in Psychoanalytic Doctrine' was published in Scilicet, 5 (1975), pp. 91–104.

During her sexual evolution, the little girl must, according to Freud, resolve two problems, whose analytic formulation he first advanced after he had noticed that this evolution comprises a time, or stage, during which everything happens for the girl exactly as it does for the boy.

This similarity indicates:

(1) that it is the mother who is the object of her desire[1] while rivalry, or the death wish, falls on the father;
(2) that equally for the girl, the only organ or, to be more precise, the only kind of sexual organ which exists is the phallus – which, as Freud makes clear, does not mean the penis, unless we were to talk of a penis with the remarkable characteristic of not admitting to a vagina. This point is worth stopping at.

It is of course obvious that the idea of an organ in glorious, monadic isolation, rejecting any tie or relation (whether complementary or antagonistic) in favour of the sole alternative of being or of not being, must refer to an essentially imaginary organ, even if this image is that of a real organ, namely the penis, or, more precisely, the penis in its privileged state of tumescence and erection.

Secondly, it is no less obvious that the playing out of this alternative must bring about a subtle nuancing of the category of sex or of the other sex, even before it has appeared. For beings are to be divided up, not into men and women or males and females, but only into those who have the phallus and those who do not, meaning in this last case (since only the phallus exists) those who are castrated, or rather, eunuchs. Where, then, should we look for the woman?

One look at common parlance or common modes of reasoning is enough to establish that the phallic division cannot be superimposed onto sexual division. For example, a certain society might decide to make a certain activity, quality or distinguishing mark a characteristic of man or of woman, that is, a difference according to which men and women should be recognised. There will always be one woman, not incidentally lacking in supporters, to show that this difference is no difference: for instance, a woman learned in Greek, in a society which restricts the study of this language to young boys, as was indeed the case during the Renaissance. But the point of this effective demonstration is always missed, for instead of admitting that being a woman is no handicap for learning Greek – which after all has no need of demonstration – it is concluded that because she is learned in Greek she must be a man. Furthermore, women are not second to men in this kind of reasoning. What is more common than to hear our women analysands expressing the fear that by becoming 'theoreticians' they cease to be women? It is not enough simply not to be a feminist to ensure that one knows one's place in the business of sex.

If, therefore, it is the case that, contrary to all common sense, phallicism, or the belief in one single type of sexual organ, is the one thing in the world most equally shared between the sexes, and if there is only one basic form of incest – that which takes the mother as its object – then two problems clearly arise for the girl which the boy is spared, one of which concerns her relation to the object, and the other her relation to her own body.

For while the boy must of course give up the first object of his desire, it is for another woman; whereas the girl must manage the same renunciation for the sake of an object of the opposite sex. Likewise, both before and after this renunciation, the phallus remains, so to speak, on the side of the boy; the girl first thinks that it can be found in that part of her body bearing the closest resemblance to its form, that is, the clitoris, and then has to give up her investment in this erotogenic zone in favour of the vagina. Freud even goes so far as to make the criterion for the successful sexual normativisation of the woman a restricting of orgasm to the vaginal orgasm alone. This calls for a number of wide-ranging remarks, but it is a crucial issue which has been fiercely debated within analytic doctrine.

In actual fact, according to this criterion, all the evidence goes to show that the normal woman is a somewhat rare phenomenon, and, when we do come across her, it would seem that she does not stand out as a model of normality. I am saying 'it would seem' because my reference is to recently published case-studies, whose author, following the method dear to the United States, proceeds by way of correlations established by the most dubious of methods – dubious, that is, for everyone except the author, who believes, with disarming naïvety, that he is 'letting the facts speak' for themselves.[2] Nothing stops us, however, from making the most remarkable findings in a collection of this kind, such as the fact that women who have exclusively vaginal orgasms show a strongly marked propensity to anxiety. An observation for what it's worth, but which is by no means indispensable, since the fictive nature of the criterion laid down by Freud is obvious without this false appeal to 'scientific data'. So is this a case of prejudice on the part of Freud? One thing we can be sure of, there is a theoretical reason involved which is in urgent need of clarification.

In point of fact, phallicism for the girl has always seemed difficult to explain, if not incredible. What tends to be overlooked is that it is no less so in the case of the boy. It only *appears* more easy to explain in his case, and I would argue that this apparent ease is a function of phallicism itself. So how does Freud explain it for the boy?

According to Freud, the boy manages from a very early age to distinguish between men and women by going on all kinds of indications, clothes in particular, without it occurring to him to relate these perceived differences on which he bases his distinction to a difference between the genital organs of the two parties. This is due to his ignorance, since at that stage he has had no chance of observing the anatomical distinction between the two sexes. Not that he reserves judgement for all that – for him, everyone is equipped with a phallus. Why? This is where his narcissism comes in. Such is the importance which the little boy attaches to an organ which is so rich in sensations and whose significance he obscurely grasps, that he loves himself precisely as a boy. One might as well say, even if Freud doesn't do so explicitly, that from then on narcissism can only work on this condition, that the little boy does, or does not, love himself according to whether he is sufficiently in possession of the phallus or not. From that point, the very idea that this organ might be lacking becomes intolerable to him. In defiance of his sexed being, for want of a better expression, he imagines everyone to be made in his own image, that is, in his image such as he loves it. If we now assume the existence of an analogous organ for the girl, and take this to be the clitoris, which acquires the same importance for her as the condition for her loving herself, then an identical explanation would be made a lot easier. Only, is such an explanation tenable?

As far as the boy's ignorance is concerned, a young boy can be seen to have very early visual access to a differently made body from his own, such as that of a mother with few scruples about having her bath in front of him, or a sister dressed and undressed before his eyes. This won't stop things from proceeding for him in exactly the same way, meaning that at no point is his relation to anything which might be termed an other sex, but only to a covering . . . behind which it is impossible for there not to be a phallus. Thus ignorance can explain nothing, since knowledge, the lifting of this ignorance, is no obstacle to occult science. As for narcissism, are we providing an explanation or merely setting up the most inscrutable of enigmas when we talk of a love of self which implies one's own liquidation as sexed being?

The fact remains, however, that the enigma is there, in that whatever the sex of the subject, the only conceivable pleasure in his or her image depends on finding in that image or thinking that he or she finds there (which means if only in the mind) something withdrawn from sight which answers or corresponds to what we have called the monadic phallus. Narcissism is henceforth a 'phallo-narcissism', which means, and the expression has no other meaning, that the subject loves himself or herself as phallus, in the two senses that grammatical analysis gives to this phrase. Once this fact has been put like this, we are in a position to throw some light on a famous quarrel.

In point of fact, when Karen Horney disputes the anatomical priority of the clitoris, which according to Freud, is facilitated by its being within reach of the girl's knowledge and her hand, and when she states that the girl knows of the existence of the vagina, for our part we see no reason to disagree. Only this in no sense detracts from Freud's basic thesis on the phallic conditioning of narcissism in the subject irrespective of its sex, a thesis which no direct observation could either invalidate or confirm, since it is established in, and only in, analytic practice. So-called 'direct' observation is as useless here as it is in relation to the Oedipus complex. For example, one may think one is 'ascertaining' Oedipal desire on hearing a child say to its mother: 'When I grow up, I will marry you.' Whereas, in saying this, the child is simply on the way to becoming more stupid than a half-wit, by giving in to the presence of a maternal desire felt by the child as overwhelming. The field of analytic experience is not that of perception – the perception the subject might have of anatomical difference. Nor is it that of consciousness – the consciousness the subject gains of his or her sex as a boy or girl on the basis of that perception. Its field is that of the thought which slides between perception and consciousness. This is where Freud situates himself, unlike Karen Horney, analyst as she claims to be. And that alone refutes all her objections and gives them their true weight as mere quibbles. What, then, does analytic experience alone teach us?

In some female patients the clitoris does indeed function as the fantasmatic equivalent of a 'little penis' and such cases were certainly not foreign to Freud's thesis. But it is equally certain that other cases show us the girl remaining free, at the whim of her fantasy, to throw the phallic image back onto any other zone of her own body, not excluding the vagina which she would then think of as a hollowed-out phallus. On occasions this is proved by this fantasy of women analysands – that merely by turning inside out like a glove she would turn into the still form of her rivalry, which also represents the most intimate and inadmissable nucleus of her identity.

Where this fantasy predominates, and it comes out in subjects strongly inclined to sublimations as hazy as they are unproductive, it induces, not frigidity, but more precisely a quasi-total extinction of sexual life, except possibly in the domain of verbal parade. An extinction which the women in question are not even aware of, but which strikes them as quite normal, that is, as belonging in the order of things. In short, they do not see it as having the value of a symptom but rather as adding to their 'value'. Which makes us ask: why does the equation 'vagina = phallus or hollowed-out phallus' give rise to a half-unsuspected, half-tolerated frigidity, whereas the equation 'clitoris = little penis' detracts nothing from the sensitivity of this part of the body, to which, what is more, erotogenicity tends to become confined?

The only answer to this question I can think of is that the two equations or two identities have neither the same meaning nor the same weight. The equation 'vagina = hollowed-out phallus' involves, at the level of fantasy or belief, such a reduction of the phallic image to one's own body, or to that particular region of the body, that the subject no longer hesitates, so to speak, to draw the inference. Her desire is then reabsorbed into the sole desire of displaying 'it', as was the case of the little girl reported by Anna Freud in her work, *The Ego and the Mechanisms of Defence* [1937, pp. 92–3]. This type of case shows the subject of the female sex so convinced of having it that one starts to wonder whether one can still talk of a division of the subject; the least that one can note is that there is no apparent division. And it is precisely this abolition of sexual life, which threatens to come about with the abolition of lack, that incites certain other women to fall back on the equation 'clitoris = little penis', which, as its formula indicates ('little penis'), leaves the field open, if you will pardon the expression, to some hope. There is, however, a close link between this equation and the first, which can be sensed in the worry, not to say the genuine 'state' that the woman gets into over her vaginal frigidity. This is especially so when, as is often the case nowadays, she is familiar with what has become the commonplace Freudian thesis that elimination of clitoral orgasm is the criterion of femininity, or of the woman's successful sexual normativisation – which doesn't make our task as analysts any easier. Freud, that is, Freud himself, demands that the woman analysand comes – vaginally. Hardly an injunction to which it would be easy to respond; indeed, on the contrary, it can only reinforce, in some cases *beyond recovery* [English in the original], a purely anal subjective integration of sexuality. It is hardly surprising that analysts, notably Helene Deutsch, are stressing more and more the resistance of an increasingly widespread clitoral fixation to all therapeutic efforts.

The preceding outline will not, I hope seem too long in relation to the conclusion that I wish to draw from it – that while the erotogenicity of the vagina strikes me no more as a sign of normality than that of the clitoris a sign of abnormality, the fact none the less remains that frigidity constitutes a definite symptomatic disturbance of sexual life in the woman, in the full psychoanalytic sense of the term symptom. I am deliberately avoiding the term orgasm, which raises problems too complex to be dealt with here. We need only think back to the observations of Masters and Johnson, which I consider to be highly dubious, and to the bold conclusions – to say the least – which Mary Jane Sherfey drew from them [Sherfey, 1966]. Without espousing all her arguments, I would concede to this author that the transference of orgasmic capacity from the clitoris to the vagina is a mythical concept of femininity, even from the biological point of view. From the point of view of psychoanalysis, what matters is not the transformation of the clitoral into the vaginal, but that of auto-erotic libido into object libido. Both girl and boy have to undergo a double renunciation: of the mother, on the one hand, of masturbation, on the other. The only feature which is specific to the sexual evolution of the girl resides in her directing her desire towards an object of a different sex to her mother. How does she make this step? In other words, how does she enter into the specifically feminine Oedipus complex?

To answer this question, Freud says that we must start by examining the nature of the ties attaching the girl to her mother, which does seem the correct way to proceed. What does the little girl want from her mother? Or again, what does she demand of her? That is the key question, whose answer is the precondition for solving the problem. But, as the father of psychoanalysis goes on to add, this is precisely where we find ourselves in a region where everything is cloaked in obscurity. The ties in question seem to have succumbed to such an inexorable repression and to belong to such a far-off and deeply buried epoch, that we will no doubt have to wait for the results of later investigations before any light can be shed on this 'dark continent'.

Now, the fact of the matter is that later investigations have not produced the clarification that Freud hoped for, and they have failed to do so precisely to the extent that they have been carried out along the paths traced by Freud's dearly loved metaphors (which I would call archaeological). To devote oneself to such investigations with the naïve idea that one will discover something if one only goes back far enough, as if desire were daughter of an epoch, is a blind alley. It can only lead away from the understanding dawning on anyone who has the not so naïve idea of pondering on the very wording of the question. I am thinking of Lacan, since it is he who has brought out the full impact of Freud's question.

'What does the little girl demand of her mother?' But it's easy! She has no shortage of words for telling us: to dress her, to make her hurt go away, to take her for a walk, to belong to her, or to her alone, in short all sorts of demands, including at times the demand to leave her alone, that is, the demand to take a rest from all demand. If, therefore, Freud's question has any meaning, it must signify something else, that is, not so much 'What is she demanding *of her*?', as 'What is she *demanding*, what is she really demanding, by demanding of her mother all that?'

In other words, Freud's question implies the separating out of demand onto two planes: that of the demands effectively spoken, or enounced, and that of Demand (with a capital D) which subsists within and beyond these very demands, and which, because it remains resistant to articulation, incites the little girl to make those demands at the same time as rendering them futile, both the demands and any reply they might receive.

Is it desire? – this Demand, this unknown Demand, which language does not allow to be spoken and for which there are no words. Definitely not. Freud's question can be put either of two ways: what does the little girl *demand* of her mother or what does she *want* from her? It refers, therefore, to a field appearing first as the field of a pure and empty want, one which is not yet inhabited unless it be by the very idea of the Thing, the Thing on which Freud is interrogating the little girl by asking her what she wants. As we will see, desire is precisely what comes to inhabit this field of empty want. By inhabiting this field as the Thing itself, it takes on the structure of demand. Not that this makes it into a demand, since this coming of the Thing does not necessarily leave the subject in a position to say what thing it is. A thing in itself, a thing with its mouth sealed. How does this Thing come into being? How does desire come to inhabit this field?

Here we need to make a fairly simple point: that the question of what she wants is as much the question of the girl herself as it is that of the Other, whether this be Freud, ourselves, or again and in the first instance, the Mother. It is, therefore, a question which can apparently be formulated either way, as 'What do I want?', or as 'What do you want?' In fact only the second formula is tenable. For in the last analysis, what is involved is a question which comes to her as in echo to her own demand. At the moment when she says 'milk' or 'it hurts' or 'walk', at that very moment the question resounds back to her from the place from which she draws these functional signifiers, in the form 'what do you want?' The 'you' descends on her with no possibility of error, since it is a 'you' not addressed to her as a person or as second person, but one which strikes her at the very roots of her want. There is no 'you' unless it comes from the Other with a capital O. Once the little girl is in a position to receive its message in the inverted form of 'I', once she can refer to her image with this 'I' and effectively articulate the question 'What do I want?', then she is already in the realm of 'intersubjectivity', which may soon become that of 'personalism', but which in any case is beyond the pale.

If we, on the other hand, stay on this side of it, it is easy to see that what we have just stated can be written as the question mark of Lacan's graph[3] (reproduced below).

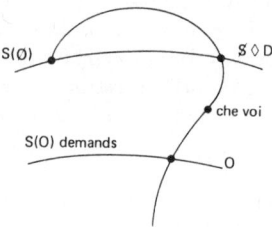

I had reached the point in my argument when the girl finds herself barred in the face of Demand. To be *Barred* means to have no possibility of saying which demand. The result is that she can only constitute herself as not-knowing. In so far as she is not purely and simply reduced to what is designated at the time as 'I', in the statements which unfold along the bottom line, that is, to the pure claim of being there, then the girl speeds, so to speak, towards the line above, where we rediscover her as subject,' but as a subject which does not know. This implies that knowledge is presupposed – or even posed. The reply *is*, because there is the question. And it is somewhere other than in the subject, in another place: the place of the Other where the question mark comes to an end.

But it only needs someone, not excluding our little girl turned chatterbox, to put themselves in this place and from there to strive to answer, for them to discover that their reply necessarily misses the point. The only valid way of filling this place is to hold on, as Freud did, to the question itself – what does she want? Is there anything more ridiculous than hearing an analyst express his regret, or fear, that the conditions of our century are standing in the way of woman's natural fulfilment, her true desire for maternity (Nacht, 1973)? If we can be so sure that this is woman's desire or the desire of every woman, then why not go and open a marriage counsel bureau or practice artificial insemination instead of bothering with psychoanalysis? The anguish of such analysts will not blind us to the fact that no answer could be the Answer. The Other is barred, just as much as the girl. The Other of truth *is-without* truth. Truth is involved only in so far as it is excluded from the utterance and simultaneously declares it false. Corresponding to the message on the bottom line of statements [*énoncés*], there is, on the line of enunciation [*énonciation*] above, an 'I am lying'. But, surely this undermines the very possibility of speaking since I can say nothing, not even a lie, without believing in it a little. And then, what is there to say? What is there to want when want persists as pure want? We are back to our earlier question in a slightly different form: how has a desire come to inhabit this field of pure want, at the moment when the subject starts to speak?

Our argument will be easier to follow here if we appeal to an experience, one which is moreover fairly banal. The experience we go through, for example, when we want to buy a piece of antique furniture. Who will authenticate it? The dealer's word is not gospel. We therefore need a stamp to guarantee both the good faith of the dealer and that of the piece of furniture. It is a rescindable guarantee, since we can ask whether it is false; it is even useless, since not all pieces of antique furniture are necessarily stamped. Not that this stops us from demanding it; and the demand couldn't have arisen were it not laid down somewhere, whether explicitly or not, that no piece of furniture can guarantee its own authenticity.

Imagine now a piece of furniture which, struck by this inability to certify its own authenticity, lights on the idea of the stamp, which the other pieces of furniture, its neighbours in the same gallery, seem equally deprived of – its feeling would be one of irremediable loss. But it would only need one piece of furniture to bear the stamp for the situation of all the others to change completely. Each one would rig itself out with the same stamp and from then on, like the table Marx talks about in one of the first chapters of *Capital*, would never tire of the oratorial flight in which it sings out its own exchange value, its use value incidentally remaining unaltered.

It is obvious what this fable is about – nothing less than the experience of our being or of what we are, for none of us are dispensed from thinking of ourselves as a piece of furniture. It is Lacan who first brought to light the effects which demand has in bringing whoever articulates it, even if they are a piece of furniture, up against a place which is the place of language and of Truth (with a capital T). Only by examining these effects, has it

at last become possible to dispel the mystery surrounding the
phallic function, which is the most disturbing of all functions,
and not only for the analysts (but above all for the analysts). Here
we leave the plane of deduction for that of analytic experience.
And what, precisely, does this experience teach us about the
phallus, if not that it makes a joke of phallicism? The phallicism
which extends to those theories which ring out like so many
empty hymns in praise of the divine phallus, of the phallus as the
symbol of life, of creation or procreation, or as a symbol of the
unity and cohesion of the body, etc. To be more rigorous, what
is the phallus if not that which renders vain and derisory the
regressive positionings of the ego ideal, which start from the
ideal ego, whether these positions are oral, anal or phallic? In
other words, the phallus is the very point where the Other of
Truth (capital T) is seen to be without truth (small t); at which
point, precisely, objects start performing like stamps. These
objects are taken from the body itself. For what is the pheno-
menal being of the subject, if not to all intents and purposes a
body? And what, therefore, could be the subject's noumenal
being, if not that aspect of the same body which remains invisible
to the subject? At the moment when the subject articulates the
first demands, the field of pure want has already been transformed by these objects into the field of the drives: $\$ \lozenge D$.

How does this phallic function come into play? That much we
know – who hasn't heard of the paternal metaphor? What we
perhaps don't know so well is the link between this effect of the
paternal metaphor and the production of a lying subject, that is,
of a subject who is marked with a bar which refutes any ontology.

Why does this indication (that the Other is barred) take on an
imaginary form, and especially a form drawn from the most
salient and, so to speak, the most conspicuous organ of procreation? For the moment the important thing to note is that if
the function of this phallus ($- \Phi$), which we lend wings to not
only on account of its erectibility, is an undeniable fact of Freud's
experience, this fact stands less in the way of our understanding
as soon as it is related, not to the sex of the girl but to her status or
condition as speaking subject. The problem then is that the same
function has to be explained similarly or along the same lines for
the boy: since he too shares that condition.

Thus our puzzlement has turned inside out or almost. The

question of how it can be the case that the girl experiences the same phallicism as the boy hands over to the question of what it can still mean for them to call themselves boy or girl, or, to be more precise (since they don't call themselves boy or girl so much as repeat it) for us to call them different. An additional question to the one which was set aside but not forgotten in the course of the argument, that is, how does the little girl manage to transfer, not the erotogenicity of the clitoris to the vagina, but her desire or preference to an object of another sex to that of her mother?

It seems to me that the correct procedure would be to take up the second question first, which is a task I will have to come back to later. For the moment, I should just point out that as a preliminary it calls for a revision of Freud's theses on the dissolution of the Oedipus complex, as well as a close examination of what he calls the appearance of the one or the single object during the period of early or infantile sexuality, and also of the way in which the boy himself struggles with the phallicism which appears at this same period. My objective in this article, intended after all only as an introduction, was simply to show: *first*, that phallicism is an 'unconscious phenomenon', if this somewhat risky expression be permitted, which has nothing natural about it for the boy any more so than for the girl, and to show, *secondly*, the common root of the phallic function in its relation to discourse. This path, marked out by Lacan, could already be glimpsed in the ancient paradox of the phallus, which appeared alternatively as the principle of madness and of reason.

If this objective has been achieved, as I hope it has, it should enable us to dispense with a certain number of questions, such as the following:

There is a book which came out recently under the title *Woman as Sex Object* (Hess and Nochlin, 1973). It is a collective work whose authors, mostly women, are all art historians. The central idea of this work consists of noting that it has been men, or almost exclusively men, in modern times at least, who have produced and elaborated at all levels, from the pornographic photo to high art, what the authors call the common places of desire – a reference not to brothels, but to dead metaphors such as eyes in the shapes of cups or fountains, cherry lips or apple breasts, etc. This to such an extent that it is redundant to speak of *masculine* eroticism or *feminine* object, and equally for the authors to regret the fact that women, whether this be their doing or that of the men, have not had the same opportunity to elaborate the common places of their desire. The basic question which I would like to put to these authors is the following: can one speak of the common places, the *topoi*, of a desire which might be feminine?

Notes

1. Not to be confused, as Strachey thinks, with the object 'of her love'; cf. his note (Freud, XIX, 1925, p. 246), to the effect that this was not an entirely new discovery by Freud, since he had said in the *Three Essays* that the girl's first love-object was her mother.
2. Fisher (1973), in which we equally learn that college girls have more highly developed orgasmic capacities than their maids, and than the women workers employed by their fathers.
3. The graph is a modified version of the graph given in four stages in 'Subversion of the Subject and Dialectic of Desire' (*Ecrits*, (1960)). It represents the radical division/inversion which constitutes the subject in its relation to the signifying chain – division between the subject of the enunciated (the demands it utters) and the subject of the enunciation (its fading before the very process of demand); inversion of the query which the subject sees as emanating from the Other ('What do you want?') and which the subject must reverse or take up in its own place ('What does it want from me?') (tr.).

CHAPTER SIX

God and the *Jouissance*
of ~~The~~ Woman.
A Love Letter

Undoubtedly the most controversial and difficult of the texts in this collection, 'God and the Jouissance *of ~~The~~ Woman' and 'A Love Letter' are the two central chapters of Lacan's* Seminar XX, Encore, *which he gave in 1972–3.*

In relation to the previous articles, Encore *marks a turning point in Lacan's work, both at the conceptual level and in terms of its polemic. It represents Lacan's most direct attempt to take up the question of feminine sexuality, not just as part of a return to the earlier debate, but in a way which goes beyond Freud. And it raises issues which clearly relate to feminist demands for an understanding of femininity which is not confined by the phallic definition.*

It is the central tenet of these chapters that 'The Woman' does not exist, in that phallic sexuality assigns her to a position of fantasy. Lacan argues that the sexual relation hangs on a fantasy of oneness, which the woman has classically come to support. He traces that fantasy through a sustained critique of courtly, religious and ethical discourse.

Against this fantasy, Lacan sets the concept of jouissance. *Jouissance is used here to refer to that moment of sexuality which is always in excess, something over and above the phallic term which is the mark of sexual identity. The question Lacan explicitly asks is that of woman's relation to* jouissance. *It is a question which can easily lapse into a mystification of woman as the site of truth.*

This is why Lacan's statements in Encore, *on the one hand, have been accused of being complicit with the fantasy they try to expose, and, on the other, have led to attempts to take the 'otherness' of femininity even further, beyond the limits of language which still forms the basis of Lacan's account.*

These chapters – which show 'Woman' as a category constructed around the phallic term at the same time as they slip into the question of her essence – underline the problem which has dominated the psycho-

analytic debate on feminine sexuality to date: how to hold on to Freud's most radical insight that sexual difference is a symbolic construct; how to retrieve femininity from a total subordination to the effects of that construction.

The cultural references in this text are especially dense. But rather than weigh down the text with references, we have chosen to leave the various allusions to work in terms of how they are used in the course of Lacan's argument.

'God and the Jouissance *of The Woman' and 'A Love Letter' are Chapters 6 and 7 of* Seminar XX, Encore *(Lacan, 1972–3), pp. 61–82.*

GOD AND THE *JOUISSANCE* OF THE WOMAN

> [Reading-loving, hating][1]
> The materialists
> Jouissance of being
> The male, polymorphous pervert
> The mystics

2

Today I will be elaborating the consequences of the fact that in the case of the speaking being the relation between the sexes does not take place, since it is only on this basis that what makes up for that relation can be stated.

For a long time now I have laid down with a certain *There is something of One* the first step of this undertaking. This *There is something of One* is not simple – to say the least. In psychoanalysis, or more precisely in the discourse of Freud, it is set forth in the concept of Eros, defined as a fusion making one out of two, that is, of Eros seen as the gradual tendency to make one out of a vast multitude. But, just as it is clear that even all of you, while undoubtedly you are here a multitude, not only do not make one but have no chance of so doing – as is shown only too clearly, and that every day, if only by communing in my speech – so Freud had to raise up another factor as obstacle to this universal Eros, in the shape of Thanatos, which is the reduction to dust.

Clearly this is a metaphor allowed to Freud by the fortunate discovery of the two units of the germen, the ova and the spermatazoa, whose fusion, crudely speaking, engenders – what? a new being. With this qualification, that the thing does not come about without a meiosis, a quite manifest subtraction for at least one of the two just before the conjunction is effected, a subtraction of certain elements which are not without their place in the final operation.

We can, however, comfort ourselves that there is unquestionably much less of the biological metaphor here than elsewhere. If the unconscious is indeed what I say it is, as being structured like a language, then it is on the level of language that we must interrogate this One. This One has resounded endlessly across the centuries. Need I bother to evoke here the neo-platonists? Perhaps I should very briefly mention that whole saga, but later, since my task today is to make clear exactly how this issue not only can, but must, be addressed from within our discourse, and from the new perspective which our experience opens up in the domain of Eros.

We must start on the basis that this *There is something of One* is to be taken with the stress that there is One alone. Only thus can we grasp the nerve of the thing called love, since we too must call it by the name under which it has echoed across the centuries. In analysis we are dealing only with this thing, and it comes into play through no other path. It is a strange path which in itself enabled me to isolate something I felt myself bound to uphold in the transference, inasmuch as this is indistinguishable from love, by means of the formula: *the subject supposed to know*.

I cannot avoid stressing the new resonance which this term, to know, might take on for you. He whom I suppose to know, I love. Earlier you saw me wavering, drawing back, hesitating to come down on the side of one meaning or the other, on the side of love or of what is called hate, when I urged you to share in a reading whose express objective is to discredit me – which should hardly deter someone who speaks of nothing but disabusement, and who aims at nothing less. The point is that what makes this objective seem tenable for the authors is a de-supposition of my knowledge. When I say that they hate me, what I mean is that they de-suppose me of knowledge.

And why not indeed? Why not, if it transpires that this is the precondition of what I call a reading? After all, what can I presume of what Aristotle knew? Possibly I might read him better the less of this knowledge I suppose him to have. Such is the condition of a strict test of reading, and it is the one condition which I do not let myself off.

We cannot ignore what is there for us to read in that part of language which exists – namely, what turns out to form a weave by way of its precipitous ups and downs (which is how I define writing). It would, therefore, be disdainful not to give some echo at least to what has been elaborated through the ages on the subject of love, by a thinking which has been termed – incorrectly I might say – philosophical.

This is not the place for a general review of the question. Given the kind of faces which I see blurred before me, I would judge you to have heard that within philosophy the love of God has held a certain place. This is a fact of great import which, if only indirectly, psychoanalytic discourse cannot afford to ignore.

Which reminds me of something which was said when I was excluded, as they put it in this little book, from Saint Anne.[2] As it happens, I was not excluded, I withdrew, which is very different, not that it matters, since that is hardly the issue, especially as the term 'excluded' has its own importance in my topology. Some well-meaning people – always worse than those who mean badly – were surprised to have it reach them that I placed between man and woman a certain Other who seemed remarkably like the good old God of all times. They only heard it indirectly and became the willing bearers of the tidings. And my God, to put it aptly, these people belonged to the pure philosophical tradition, from among those who lay claim to materialism – which is precisely why I call it pure, since there is nothing more philosophical than materialism. Materialism feels itself obliged, God knows why, we can appropriately say, to be on guard against this God whom I have said to have dominated in philosophy the whole debate about love. Hence these people, to whose warm intervention I owed a replenished audience, were somewhat put out.

For my part, it seems plain that the Other, put forward at the time of 'The Agency of the Letter' (*Ecrits*, (1957)), as the place of speech, was a way, I can't say of laicising, but of exorcising our good old God. After all, there are many people who compliment me for having managed to establish in one of my last seminars that God does not exist. Obviously they hear – they hear, but unfortunately they understand, and what they understand is a little hasty.

Today, however, my objective is rather to show you precisely in what he exists, this good old God. The mode in which he exists may well not please everyone, especially not the theologians who, as I have been saying for a long time, are far more capable than I am of doing without his existence. Unfortunately I am not quite in the same position because I am dealing with the Other. This Other, while it may be one alone, must have some relation to what appears of the other sex.

In this context, during the year of the 'Ethics of Psychoanalysis' (SVII), which I referred to last time, I did not desist from referring to courtly love. What is it?

It is an altogether refined way of making up for the absence of sexual relation by pretending that it is we who put an obstacle to it. It is truly the most staggering thing that has ever been tried. But how can we expose its fraud?

Instead of wavering over the paradox that courtly love appeared in the age of feudalism, the materialists should see this as a magnificent opportunity for showing how, on the contrary, it is rooted in the discourse of fealty, of fidelity to the person. In the last resort, the person is always the discourse of the master. For the man, whose lady was entirely, in the most servile sense of the term, his female subject, courtly love is the only way of coming off elegantly from the absence of sexual relation.

It is along these lines that later I will be dealing with the notion of the obstacle – later, since today I have a certain area to work on – the area which in Aristotle (for all that, I do prefer Aristotle to Geoffrey Rudel) is precisely called the obstacle, the ἔνστασις.

[. . . .]

If you consult Aristotle, everything will be clear to you when I finally take up this issue of the ἔνστασις. You could then go on to read the piece from the *Rhetoric* and the two pieces from the *Topics* which will enable you to grasp exactly what I am getting at when I try to reintegrate into Aristotle my four formulas, the ∃x.Φ͞x and so on.

Finally, as a last point on the subject, why should the materialists, as we call them, be indignant that I place God as third party, and why not, in this affair of human love? After all, doesn't it ever happen, even to materialists, to know something about the *ménage à trois*?

So let us try to proceed. Proceed on the basis of this fact that there is no evidence that I do not know what I am meant to be saying when I am speaking to you here. What puts this book on the wrong track from start to finish is that they suppose me – after which anything is possible – they suppose me to have an ontology, or, what amounts to the same thing, a system.

[. . . .]

And yet it is, surely, unequivocal that, as against the being upheld by philosophical tradition, that is, the being residing in thought and taken to be its correlate, I argue that we are played by *jouissance*.

Thought is *jouissance*. What analytic discourse brings out is this fact, which was already intimated in the philosophy of being – that there is a *jouissance* of being.

If I spoke to you about the *Nicomachean Ethics*, it was precisely because a hint of this is there. Aristotle's endeavour, and it opened the path to everything that followed in his train, was to discover what is *jouissance* of being. Someone like Saint Thomas then had no difficulty in forging out of this the physical theory of love as it was called by Abbot Rousselot – which is that, all things considered, the first being of which we are aware is that of our own being, and everything which is for our own good will, by dint of that fact, be *jouissance* of the supreme Being, that is, of God. In short, in loving God it is ourselves we love, and by first loving ourselves – a convenient charity as they say – we render to God the appropriate homage.

The being – if I absolutely must use the term – the being I set against this is the being of *signifiance*. And I fail to see how it can be construed as a betrayal of the ideals of materialism – I say the *ideals* because it falls outside the limits of its conceptual design – to recognise that the motive of this being of *signifiance* lies in *jouissance*, *jouissance* of the body.

But then you see, ever since Democritus, a body has not seemed sufficiently materialist. You have to have atoms, and the whole works, sight and smell and everything that follows. It all absolutely hangs together.

It is not fortuitous that at times Aristotle quotes Democritus, even if he feigns disgust, since he based himself on him. In point of fact, the atom is simply a floating element of *signifiance*, quite simply a στοιχεῖον. Except that you get into real trouble if you only retain what makes the element elementary, that is, the fact that it is unique, when what we need to bring in a little is the other, that is, difference.

Now then, this *jouissance* of the body. If there is no sexual relation, we need to see, in that relation, what purpose it might serve.

3

Let's start on the side where all x is a function of Φx, that is, on the side of the man.

On the whole one takes up this side by choice – women being free to do so if they so choose. Everyone knows that there are phallic women and that the phallic function does not prevent men from being homosexual. But at the same time it is this function which enables them to situate themselves as men, and to take on the woman. I will deal briefly with man, because what I want to talk about today is the woman and I presume I have sufficiently drummed it into you for you still to have it in your heads – that, short of castration, that is, short of something which says no to the phallic function, man has no chance of enjoying the body of the woman, in other words, of making love.

That is the conclusion of analytic experience. It does not stop him from desiring the woman in any number of ways, even when this condition is not fulfilled. Not only does he desire her but he does all kinds of things to her which bear a remarkable resemblance to love.

Contrary to what Freud argues, it is the man – by which I mean he who finds himself male without knowing what to do about it, for all that he is a speaking being – who takes on the woman, or who can believe he takes her on, since on this question con-victions, those I referred to last time as con-victions,[3] are not wanting. Except that what he takes on is the cause of his desire, the cause I have designated as the *objet a*. That is the act of love. To make love, as the term indicates, is poetry. Only there is a world between poetry and the act. The act of love is the polymorphous perversion of the male, in the case of the speaking being. There is nothing more emphatic, more coherent or more strict as far as Freudian discourse is concerned.

I have half an hour left to try to introduce you, if I dare so express myself, to what is involved on the side of the woman. Well, it is either one thing or the other – either what I write has no meaning, or when I write $\overline{\forall x}\Phi x$, this hitherto unstated function in which the negation bears on the quantifier to be read as *not all*, it means that when any speaking being whatever lines up under the banner of women it is by being constituted as not all that they are placed within the phallic function. It is this that defines the . . . the what? – the woman precisely, except that *The* woman can only be written with *The* crossed through. There is no such thing as *The* woman, where the definite article stands for the universal. There is no such thing as *The* woman since of her essence – having already risked the term, why think twice about it? – of her essence, she is not all.

[. . . .]

More than one of my pupils have got into a mess about the lack of the signifier, the signifier of the lack of the signifier, and other muddles regarding the phallus, whereas what I am pointing to with this *the*[4] is the signifier, which is after all common and even indispensable. The proof is that earlier on I was already talking about man and *the* woman. This *the* is a signifier. It is by means of this *the* that I symbolise the signifier whose place must be marked and which cannot be left empty. This *the* is a signifier characterised by being the only signifier which cannot signify anything, but which merely constitutes the status of *the* woman as being not all. Which forbids our speaking of *The* woman.

There is woman only as excluded by the nature of things which is the nature of words, and it has to be said that if there is one thing they themselves are complaining about enough at the moment, it is well and truly that – only they don't know what they are saying, which is all the difference between them and me.

It none the less remains that if she is excluded by the nature of things, it is precisely that in being not all, she has, in relation to what the phallic function designates of *jouissance*, a supplementary *jouissance*.

Note that I said *supplementary*. Had I said *complementary*, where would we be! We'd fall right back into the all.

Women hold to the *jouissance* in question – none of them hold to being not all, and my God, it would be wrong not to recognise that, contrary to what is said, it is none the less they who, for the most part, possess the men.

The common man, who is not necessarily present here although I do know quite a few, calls woman the *bourgeoise*. That is what it means. That it is he who is at heel, and not her. Ever since Rabelais we have known that the phallus, her man as she calls it, is not a matter of indifference to her. Only, and this is the whole issue, she has various ways of taking it on, this phallus, and of keeping it for herself. Her being not all in the phallic function does not mean that she is not in it at all. She is in it *not* not at all. She is right in it. But there is something more.

This something more, mind, be careful not to sound it out too fast. I can find no better way of putting it, because I am having to cut and go quickly.

There is a *jouissance*, since we are dealing with *jouissance*, a *jouissance* of the body which is, if the expression be allowed, *beyond the phallus*. That would be pretty good and it would give a different substance to the WLM [*Mouvement de libération des femmes*]. A *jouissance* beyond the phallus . . . .

You may have noticed – and naturally I am speaking to the few seeming men that I can see here and there, luckily for most I don't know them, which prevents my prejudging as regards the rest – that occasionally it can happen that there is something which shakes the women up [*secouer*], or helps them out [*secourir*]. If you look up the etymology of these two words in Bloch and Von Wartburg's *Dictionary*, which I delight in and which, I am sure, none of you even have in your libraries, you will see the relationship between them. It is not, however, something that happens by chance.

There is a *jouissance* proper to her, to this 'her' which does not exist and which signifies nothing. There is a *jouissance* proper to her and of which she herself may know nothing, except that she experiences it – that much she does know. She knows it of course when it happens. It does not happen to all of them.

I don't want to end up on the issue of so-called frigidity, although we have to take fashion into account as regards relationships between men and women. It's very important. Unfortunately, in Freud's discourse, as in courtly love, the whole thing is covered over with petty considerations which have caused havoc. Petty considerations about clitoral orgasm or the *jouissance* designated as best one can, the other one precisely, which I am trying to get you to along the path of logic, since, to date, there is no other.

What gives some likelihood to what I am arguing, that is, that the woman knows nothing of this *jouissance*, is that ever since we've been begging them – last time I mentioned women analysts – begging them on our knees to try to tell us about it, well, not a word! We have never managed to get anything out of them. So as best we can, we designate this *jouissance*, *vaginal*, and talk about the rear pole of the opening of the uterus and other suchlike idiocies. If it was simply that she experiences it and knows nothing of it, then we would be able to cast considerable doubt on this notorious frigidity.

This is in itself a whole theme, a literary theme, which is well worth stopping at. Ever since I was twenty I've been doing nothing other than explore philosophers on the subject of love. Naturally I didn't immediately focus on this question of love but it gradually dawned on me, precisely with Abbot Rousselot about whom I was talking earlier, and then with the whole debate about physical and spiritual love, as they are called. I gather that Gilson did not think much of that opposition. He thought that Abbot Rousselot had made a discovery which was no discovery, since the opposition was part of the problem, and love is as spiritual in Aristotle as in Saint Bernard provided one reads properly the chapters on φιλία, or friendship. Some of you here must surely know what a literary outpouring there has been on the subject – have a look at *Love and the Western World*, by Denis de Rougement, they're all at it! – and then at another one, with no less talent for it than the rest, *Eros and Agapê*, by a Protestant called Niegrens. Naturally we ended up in Christianity by inventing a God such that it is he who comes!

All the same there is a bit of a link when you read certain genuine people who might just happen to be women. I will, however, give you a hint, one which I owe to someone who had read it and very kindly brought it to me. I ensconced myself in it. I had better write up the name otherwise you won't buy it. It's Hadewijch d'Anvers, a Beguine, what we quaintly refer to as a mystic.

I am not myself using the word mystic in the same way as Péguy. The mystical is by no means that which is not political. It is something serious, which a few people teach us about, and most often women or highly gifted people like Saint John of the

Cross – since, when you are male, you don't have to put yourself on the side of ∀x⊕x. You can also put yourself on the side of not-all. There are men who are just as good as women. It does happen. And who therefore feel just as good. Despite, I won't say their phallus, despite what encumbers them on that score, they get the idea, they sense that there must be a *jouissance* which goes beyond. That is what we call a mystic.

I have already spoken about other people who felt all right on the side of the mystics, but who preferred to situate themselves on the side of the phallic function, such as Angelus Silesius. To confuse his contemplative eye with the eye with which God is looking at him must surely partake of perverse *jouissance*. As regards the Hadewijch in question, it is the same as for Saint Theresa – you only have to go and look at Bernini's statue in Rome to understand immediately that she's coming, there is no doubt about it. And what is her *jouissance*, her *coming* from? It is clear that the essential testimony of the mystics is that they are experiencing it but know nothing about it.

These mystical ejaculations are neither idle gossip nor mere verbiage, in fact they are the best thing you can read – note right at the bottom of the page, *Add the* Ecrits *of Jacques Lacan*, which is of the same order. Given which, naturally you are all going to be convinced that I believe in God. I believe in the *jouissance* of the woman in so far as it is something more, on condition that you screen off that *something more* until I have properly explained it.

What was tried at the end of the last century, at the time of Freud, by all kinds of worthy people in the circle of Charcot and the rest, was an attempt to reduce the mystical to questions of fucking. If you look carefully, that is not what it is all about. Might not this *jouissance* which one experiences and knows nothing of, be that which puts us on the path of ex-istence? And why not interpret one face of the Other, the God face, as supported by feminine *jouissance*?

Since all this comes about thanks to the being of *signifiance*, and since this being has no place other than the place of the Other which I designate with a capital O, one can see the cockeyedness of what happens. And since it is there too that the function of the father is inscribed in so far as this is the function to which castration refers, one can see that while this may not make for two Gods, nor does it make for one alone.

In other words, it is not by chance that Kierkegaard discovered existence in a little tale of seduction. It is by being castrated, by renouncing love that he believes he accedes to it. But then after all, why shouldn't Régine also have existed? This desire for a good at one remove, a good not caused by a *petit a*, perhaps it was through the intermediary of Régine that he came to it.

A LOVE LETTER (*UNE LETTRE D'ÂMOUR*)[5]

Coalescence and scission of *a* and $S(\emptyset)$
The outsidesex
To speak to no purpose
Psychoanalysis is not a cosmology
Knowledge of *jouissance*

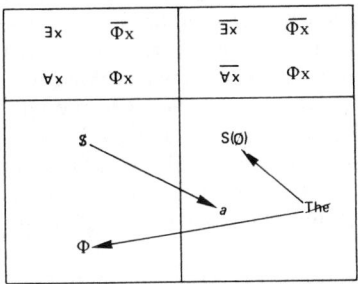

After what I have just put up on the board for you, you might think that you know it all. Don't go too fast.

Today I am going to try to talk about knowledge, the knowledge which, in the inscription of the four discourses which I think I was able to show you as underpinning the social tie, I symbolised by writing S_2. Perhaps I will manage to convey to you why this 2 goes further than being merely secondary in relation to the pure signifier which is inscribed as S_1.[6]

Since I have chosen to give you the support of this inscription on the blackboard, I will comment on it, briefly I hope. I must confess that I have nowhere written it down and nowhere prepared it. It doesn't strike me as exemplary unless it be, as usual, for producing misunderstandings.

In effect, a discourse such as analytic discourse aims at meaning. Clearly I can only deliver to each of you that part of meaning you are already on the way to absorbing. This has a limit, given by the meaning in which you are living. It is not saying too much to say that this meaning does not go very far.

What analytic discourse brings out is precisely the idea that this meaning is mere semblance.

If analytic discourse indicates this meaning to be sexual, it can only do so by taking its limits into account. There is nowhere any last word unless in the sense in which *word* is *not a word* – as I have already stressed. *No reply's the word* says la Fontaine somewhere or other. Meaning indicates the direction in which it fails.

That much established, which should keep you from understanding too fast, and having taken all the precautions dictated by prudence, or by φρόνησις, as they say in Greek – a language in which many things have been stated which none the less fall short of what analytic discourse has allowed us to articulate – here then, roughly, is what is written up on the blackboard.

First, the four propositional formulae at the top, two on the right and two on the left. Any speaking being whatever is inscribed on one side or the other. On the left, on the bottom line, $\forall x \Phi x$, indicates that it is through the phallic function that man takes up his inscription as all, except that this function finds its limit in the existence of an x through which the function, Φx, is negated $\exists x \overline{\Phi x}$. This is what is called the function of the father from where is given by negation the proposition $\overline{\Phi x}$, which allows for the exercise, through castration, of what makes up for the sexual relation – in so far as the latter can in no way be inscribed. In this case, therefore, the all rests on the exception posed as the term over that which negates this Φx totally.

Opposite, you have the inscription of the woman share of speaking beings. It is expressly stated in Freudian theory, that all speaking beings, whoever they be and whether or not they are provided with the attributes of masculinity – attributes which have yet to be determined – are allowed to inscribe themselves on this side. If they do so, they will allow of no universality, and will be that not all, in so far as there is a choice of coming down on the side of Φx, or of not being part of it.

These are the only possible definitions of the share called man, or else woman, for anyone who finds themselves in the position of inhabiting language.

Underneath, beneath the line going across where it intersects with the vertical division of what is incorrectly called humanity, inasmuch as it can be divided up into sexual identifications, you have a rough lay out of what goes on. On the side of the man, I have written up here the $, certainly not so as to privilege it in any way, and the $\emptyset$ which supports it as signifier and which can equally well be embodied by the S_1. Of all signifiers this is the signifier for which there is no signified, and which, in relation to meaning, symbolises its failing. This is the half-sense, the *inde-sense* par excellence, or if you like, the *reti-sense*. Since this $ is thus duplicated by the signifier on which basically it does not even depend, so it only ever relates as a partner to the *objet a* inscribed on the other side of the bar. It can never reach its sexual partner, which is the Other, except by way of mediation, as the cause of its desire. On this account, and as is indicated in one of my other drawings by the dotted line joining the $ and the *a*, this can only be a fantasy. This fantasy, in which the subject is caught, is the support as such of what Freudian theory explicitly calls the reality principle.

Now for the other side. This year I am taking up what Freud expressly left aside, the *Was will das Weib?* the *What does the woman want?* Freud argues that there is no libido other than masculine. Meaning what? other than that a whole field, which is hardly negligible, is thereby ignored. This is the field of all those beings who take on the status of the woman – if, indeed, this being takes on anything whatsoever of her fate. Furthermore, she is incorrectly called *the* woman, since, as I have stressed before, once the *the* of *the* woman is formulated by means of a not all, then it cannot be written. There can be no *the* here other than crossed through. This ~~The~~ relates, as I hope to show you today, to the signifier O when it is crossed through.

The Other is not only this place where truth falters. It is worth representing what the woman necessarily relates to. Certainly we only have sporadic testimonies of it, which is why I took them last time in their function as metaphor. By her being in the sexual relation radically Other, in relation to what can be said of the unconscious, the woman is that which relates to this Other. This is what I am going to try to articulate a little more precisely today.

The woman relates to the signifier of this Other, in so far as, being Other, it can only remain always Other. I can only presume here that you will think back to my statement that there is no Other of the Other. As the place where everything of the signifier which can be articulated comes to be signified, the Other is, in its very foundation, radically the Other. Which is why this signifier, with this bracket open, marks the Other as crossed through – S($\emptyset$).

How can we conceive that the Other might, somewhere, be that to which one half – since that is roughly the biological proportion – one half of speaking beings relates. And yet that is what is written up on the blackboard by means of the arrow pointing from the The. This The cannot be said. Nothing can be said of the woman. The woman relates to S($\emptyset$), which means that she is already doubled, and is not all, since on the other hand she can also relate to Φ.

Φ is assigned this phallus which I specify as being the signifier which has no signified, the signifier supported in man by phallic *jouissance*. What is it? – other than this, sufficiently stressed by the importance of masturbation in our practice, the *jouissance* of the idiot.

2

After that, to help you recover, all that remains is for me to speak to you about love. Which I will do in an instant. But what is the point of my ending up speaking to you about love, given that it scarcely follows the pretensions of analytic discourse to being something of a science.

This *something of a science* – you are hardly aware of it. Of course you are aware, since I have pointed it out to you, that there was a moment when with some justification we were able to boast that scientific discourse had been founded on the Galilean turning point. I have stressed this often enough to presume that some of you will have gone back to the sources, meaning to the work of Koyré.

In relation to scientific discourse, it is very difficult to hold equally present two terms which I will give to you now.

On the one hand, this discourse has given rise to all kinds of instruments which, from the point of view involved here, we must classify as gadgets. This makes you to a much greater extent than you are aware, the subjects of instruments which, from the microscope to the radio-television, become elements of your existence. At the present time, you cannot even measure their magnitude, but that doesn't make this any less part of what I call scientific discourse, a discourse being that which determines a form of social tie.

On the other hand, and this is where things don't jell, there is a subversion of knowledge (*connaissance*). Up till now, in relation to knowledge nothing has ever been conceived of which did not share in the fantasy of inscribing a sexual tie – and we cannot even say that the subjects of the ancient theory of knowledge were not conscious of the fact.

For example, simply take the terms active and passive which dominate everything which has ever been thought up on the relationship of form to matter, a relationship which is so fundamental and which Plato, and then Aristotle, refer to at every step they take regarding the nature of things. It is visibly, palpably the case that these propositions are only upheld by a fantasy of trying to make up for what there is no way of stating that is, the sexual relation.

The strange thing is that something, albeit something ambiguous, has none the less come out of this crude polarity, which makes matter passive and form the agency which brings to life, namely, that this bringing to life, this animation, is nothing other than the *a* whose agency animates what? – it animates nothing, it takes the other for its soul.

Look at the way that the idea of a God has progressed through the ages – not that of the Christian faith, but the God of Aristotle, the unmoved mover, the supreme sphere. The idea that there should be a being such that all lesser beings than he can have no other aim than to be as great a being as they can be, is the whole basis of the idea of Good in Aristotle's *Ethics*, which I urged you to look at so as to grasp its impasses. If we now base ourselves on the inscription on the blackboard, it becomes clear that the supreme Being, which is manifestly mythical in Aristotle, the immobile sphere from which originate all movements, whether changes, engenderings, movements, translations or whatever, is situated in the place, the opaque place of the *jouissance* of the Other – that Other which, if she existed, the woman might be.

It is in so far as her *jouissance* is radically Other that the woman has a relation to God greater than all that has been stated in ancient speculation according to a path which has manifestly been articulated only as the good of mankind.

The objective of my teaching, inasmuch as it aims at that part of analytic discourse which can be formulated, or put down, is to dissociate the *a* and the O, by reducing the former to what belongs to the imaginary and the latter to what belongs to the symbolic. That the symbolic is the support of that which was made into God, is beyond doubt. That the imaginary is supported by the reflection of like to like, is certain. And yet, *a* has come to be confused with the S(O) beneath which it is written on the board, and it has done so under pressure of the function of being. It is here that a rupture or severance is still needed. And it is in this precisely that psychoanalysis is something other than a psychology. For psychology is the non-achieving of this rupture.

3

At this point I am going to allow myself a break by reading you something I wrote for you a while back – on what? – simply from where it might be possible to speak of love.

Speaking of love, in analytic discourse, basically one does nothing else. And how could it escape us that, as regards everything that the discovery of scientific discourse has made it possible to articulate, it has been one pure and simple waste of time. What analytic discourse brings to bear – which may after all be why it emerged at a certain point of scientific discourse – is that speaking of love is in itself a *jouissance*.

This is confirmed beyond any doubt by the wholly tangible effect that by saying anything – the very rule of the discourse of the analysand – you arrive at the *Lustprinzip* (pleasure principle), and by the most direct route, without there being any need for the elevation to the higher spheres which is the basis of Aristotelian ethics.

The *Lustprinzip* can indeed only be set up through the coalescence of *a* with S(∅).

For us, of course, the O is crossed through. Which doesn't mean that it is enough to cross it through for nothing of it to exist. If I am using this S(∅) to designate nothing other than the *jouissance* of the woman, it is undoubtedly because I am thereby registering that God has not made his exit.

This is roughly what I was writing for your benefit. So what was I writing you? – the only thing one can do with a measure of seriousness, a love letter.

As far as the supposed psychologicists are concerned, thanks to whom all this has gone on for so long, I am one of those who don't do much for their reputation. And yet I fail to see why the fact of having a soul should be a scandal for thought – were it true. If it were true, the soul could only be spoken as whatever enables a being – the speaking being to call him by its name – to bear what is intolerable in its world, which presumes this soul to be alien to that world, that is to say, fantasmatic. In this world, the soul can only be contemplated through the courage and the patience with which it faces it. The proof is that up till now the soul has never had any other meaning.

At this point, *lalangue, lalangue* in French, must come to my aid – not, as is often the case, by providing me with a homonym, such as *d'eux* [of them] with *deux* [two], or *peut* [can] with *peu* [little], or take *il peut peu* [he little can] which must surely be there for a purpose – but simply by allowing me to say *on âme* [one souls]. *J'âme, tu âmes, il âme.* You can see that in this case we have to use writing, which even gives *jamais j'âmais* [never have I souled].

The soul's existence can, therefore, be placed in question [*mise en cause*] – cause being the appropriate term with which to ask if the soul be not love's effect. In effect, as long as soul souls for soul [*l'âme âme l'âme*], there is no sex in the affair. Sex does not count. The soul is conjured out of what is *hommosexual*, as is perfectly legible from history.

What I said earlier about the courage and the patience of the soul in bearing the world, is what guarantees that someone like Aristotle, in his search for the Good, stumbles on the fact that each of the beings in the world can only tend towards the greatest being by confusing their own good with that same good which radiates from the supreme Being. It is because it displays this tension towards the Supreme Being, that what Aristotle evokes as φιλία, which represents the possibility of a love tie between two of these beings, can equally be inverted in the way I expressed – that it is by their courage in bearing this intolerable relation to the supreme being that friends, φίλοι, come to recognise and choose each other. The outsidesex [*hors-sexe*] of this ethic is so evident that I would like to give it the emphasis given somewhere by Maupassant in his coinage of the strange term, *Horla*. The outsidesex [*Horsexe*], such is mankind on whom the soul did speculate.

But it can happen that women too are soulful in love [*âmour-*

euses], that is to say, that they soul for the soul. What on earth could this be other than this soul for which they soul in their partner, who is none the less *homo* right up to the hilt, from which they cannot escape? This can only bring them to the ultimate point – (ultimate not used gratuitously here) of hysteria, as it is called in Greek, or of acting the man, as I call it, thereby becoming, they too, hommosexual or outsidesex. For it is difficult for them not to sense from then on the impasse of their soully liking themselves [*se mêment*] in the Other, since after all in being Other there is no need to know that one is.

For the soul to come into being, she, the woman, is differentiated from it, and this has always been the case. Called woman [*dit-femme*] and defamed [*diffâme*]. The most famous things that have been handed down in history about women have been strictly speaking the most defamatory that could be said of them. True, the woman has been left the honour of Cornelia, the mother of the Gracchi. There's no point in talking about Cornelia to analysts, who scarcely give her a thought, but if you talk to them about any one Cornelia, they will tell you that it won't be very good for her children, the Gracchi – they'll be crack liars till the end of their days.

That was the beginning of my letter, an *âmusement*.

Earlier I made an allusion to courtly love, which appeared at the point when hommosexual *âmusement* had fallen into supreme decadence, into that sort of impossible bad dream called feudalism. In such depths of political degeneracy, it must have become noticeable that on the side of the woman, there was something which really would no longer do.

The invention of courtly love is in no sense the fruit of what history usually symbolises as the thesis–antithesis–synthesis. And of course afterwards, there was not the slightest synthesis – there never is. Courtly love blazed in history like a meteor and we have since witnessed the return of all its trappings in a so-called renaissance of the old craze. Courtly love has remained an enigma.

A brief aside – when one is made into two, there is no going back on it. It can never revert to making one again, not even a new one. The *Aufhebung* [*sublation*] is one of those sweet dreams of philosophy.

After the blazing of courtly love, it was assigned once more to its original futility by something which sprang from an entirely different quarter. It took nothing less than scientific discourse, that is, something owing nothing to the suppositions of the ancient soul.

And only this could give rise to psychoanalysis, that is, the objectification of the fact that the speaking being still spends its time speaking to no purpose. It still spends time speaking for the briefest of purposes – the briefest, I say, because it simply keeps at it, that is, for as long as is needed for the thing finally to be resolved (which is what we've got coming to us) demographically.

No way could this sort out man's relationship to women. Freud's genius was to have seen that. Freud, the very name's a laugh – *Kraft durch Freud* [*strength through Freud (joy)*] there's a programme for you. It is the most hilarious leap in the holy farce of history. Perhaps while this turning point still lasts, we might get a glimmer of something about the Other, because this is what the woman has to deal with.

I would like to add now an essential complement to something which has already been very clearly seen, but which might gain further clarification by our looking at the paths which led to that insight.

What was seen, but only from the side of the man, was that what he relates to is the *objet a*, and that the whole of his realisation in the sexual relation comes down to fantasy. It was of course seen with regard to neurotics. How do neurotics make love? That was where the whole thing started. It was impossible not to notice that there was a correlation with perversions – which lends support to my *objet a*, since, whatever the said perversions, the *a* will be there as their cause.

The funny thing is that Freud originally attributed perversions to the woman – look at the *Three Essays*. Truly a confirmation that when one is a man, one sees in one's partner what can serve, narcissistically, to act as one's own support.

Except that what came after gave ample opportunity for realising that perversions, such as one had thought to locate them in neurosis, were no such thing. Neurosis is dream rather than perversion. Neurotics have none of the characteristics of the pervert. They simply dream that they have, which is natural, since how else could they reach their partner?

It was then that one began to come across perverts – Aristotle having refused to recognise them at any price. There is in them a subversion of conduct, based on a know-how, linked to a knowledge, a knowledge of the nature of things, which leads directly from sexual conduct to its truth, namely, its amorality. Put some soul in from the start – soulmorality [*âmoralité*].

There is a morality – that is the inference – of sexual conduct. The morality of sexual conduct is implicit in everything that has ever been said about the Good.

Only, by having good to say, you end up with Kant, where morality admits to what it is. This is something which I felt needed to be argued in an article – '*Kant with Sade*' [*Ecrits*, (1963)] – morality admits it is Sade.

You can write Sade how you like – with a capital, as a tribute to the poor fool who gave us endless writings on the subject; or with a small letter, which is finally its way of being agreeable, the meaning of the word in old French; or, even better, *çade*, since it has to be said that morality stops short at the level of the *id* [*le ça*]. In other words, what it is all about is the fact that love is impossible, and that the sexual relation founders in non-sense, not that this should in any way diminish the interest we feel for the Other.

Ultimately, the question is to know, in whatever it is that constitutes feminine *jouissance* where it is not all taken up by the man – and I would even say that feminine *jouissance* as such is not taken up by him at all – the question is to know where her knowledge is at.

If the unconscious has taught us anything, it is firstly this, that somewhere, in the Other, it knows. It knows precisely because it is upheld by the signifiers through which the subject is constituted.

Now this is what makes for confusion, since it is difficult for anyone soulful not to believe that everyone in the world knows what they should be doing. If Aristotle upholds his God with that immobile sphere for all to use in pursuit of their own good, it is because this sphere is assumed to know what that good is. This is what the break induced by scientific discourse compels us to do without.

There is no need to know why. We no longer need that knowledge which Aristotle originally started out from. In order to explain the effects of gravitation, we have no need to impute to the stone a knowledge of the place where it must land. By imputing a soul to an animal, we make knowledge the pre-eminent act of nothing other than the body – note that Aristotle wasn't so wide of the mark – except that the body is made for an activity, a ἐνέργεια, and that somewhere the entelechy of the body is upheld by that substance it calls the soul.

Here analysis adds to the confusion by giving back to us the final cause, and making us state that, at least for everything concerning the speaking being, reality is of one order, that is to say, fantasmatic. How could this in any way be likely to satisfy scientific discourse?

There is, according to analytic discourse, an animal which finds himself speaking, and for whom it follows that, by inhabiting the signifier, he is its subject. From then on, everything is played out for him on the level of fantasy, but a fantasy which can perfectly well be taken apart so as to allow for the fact that he knows a great deal more than he thinks when he acts. But the fact that this is the case is not enough to give us the outlines of a cosmology.

That is the perpetual ambiguity of the term *unconscious*. Obviously the unconscious presupposes that in the speaking being there is something, somewhere, which knows more than he does, but this can hardly be allowed as a model for the world. To the extent that its possibility resides in the discourse of science, psychoanalysis is not a cosmology, although man has only to dream to see re-emerging before him that vast jumble, that lumber room he has to get by with, which doubtless makes of him a soul, and one which can be lovable when something is willing to love it.

As I have said, the woman can love in the man only the way in which he faces the knowledge he souls for. But as for the knowlege by which he is, we can only ask this question if we grant that there is something, *jouissance*, which makes it impossible to tell whether the woman can say anything about it – whether she can say what she knows of it.

At the end of today's lecture, I therefore arrive, as always, at the edge of what polarised my subject, that is, whether the question can be asked as to what she knows of it. It is no different from the question of knowing whether this end point from which she comes, which she enjoys beyond the whole game which makes up her relationship with the man, whether this point, which I call the Other signifying it with a capital O, itself knows anything. For in this she is herself subjected to the Other just as much as the man.

Does the Other know?

There was once a certain Empedocles – Freud happens to make use of him from time to time, much as a corkscrew. We only have a few lines by him, but Aristotle clearly saw what they implied when he commented that basically, for Empedocles, God was the most ignorant of all beings because he had no knowledge of hatred. Later, Christians transformed this into torrents of love. Unfortunately, it doesn't work, because to be without knowledge of hatred, is also to be without knowledge of love. If God does not know hatred, it is clear for Empedocles that he knows less than mortals.

Which might lead one to say that the more man may ascribe to the woman in confusion with God, that is, in confusion with what it is she comes from, the less he hates, the lesser he is, and since after all, there is no love without hate, the less he loves.

Notes

1. The first part of this seminar refers to *La titre de la lettre, une lecture de Lacan*, by P. Lacoue-Labarthe and J-L. Nancy (Paris: Galilée, 1973), and has been omitted in translation; wherever possible, subsequent references to this discussion have also been omitted (tr.).
2. Lacan gave his seminars at the psychiatric hospital *Saint Anne* in Paris (Centre hospitalier Saint Anne) up to the time of the split in the *Société française de psychanalyse* in 1964 (tr.).
3. The pun is on *con*, French slang for the female genitals (tr.).
4. Henceforth *the* refers to the French feminine definite article (*la*) (tr.).
5. '*Une lettre d'âmour*': throughout this section Lacan puns on *amour* (love) and *âme* (soul) – hence *une lettre d'âmour* (a love (soul) letter), love as 'soulful' in the dual sense of sexuality's relation to the mystical at the point of its excess, and of love's binding to the ethical at the point of its conventions (tr.).
6. Lacan's four discourses, introduced in his 1969–70 seminar '*L'envers de la psychanalyse*' (SXVIII) are intended to distinguish 'a certain number of stable relations in language' which go beyond 'the always more or less casual utterances of individual speech' (SXVIII, 1, p. 2), according to the place they assign to four basic units: the signifier as such (S_1), the signifying chain (S_2), the subject in its division ($\cancel{S}$), the object of desire (a). Each unit is defined by its relation to two others:

What matters is the primacy or subordination given by each form of discourse to the subject in its relation to desire. Permutation of the four basic units produces four discourses as follows (i) $\frac{S_1}{\$} \to \frac{S_2}{a}$: *discourse of the master*:

tyranny of the all-knowing and exclusion of fantasy: primacy to the signifier (S_1), retreat of subjectivity beneath its bar ($\$$), producing its knowledge as object (S_2), which stands over and against the lost object of desire (a); (ii) $\frac{S_2}{S_1} \to \frac{a}{\$}$ *discourse of the university*: knowledge in the place of the master: primacy to discourse itself constituted as knowledge (S_2), over the signifier as such (S_1), producing knowledge as the ultimate object of desire (a), over and against any question of the subject ($\$$); (iii) $\frac{\$}{a} \to \frac{S_1}{S_2}$: *discourse of the hysteric*:

the question of subjectivity: primacy to the division of the subject ($\$$), over his or her fantasy (a), producing the symptom in the place of knowledge (S_1), related to but divided from the signifying chain which supports it (S_2); (iv) $\frac{a}{S_2} \to \frac{\$}{S_1}$: *discourse of the analyst*: the question of desire: primacy to the

object of desire (a), over and against knowledge as such (S_2), producing the subject in its division ($\$$) (a→$\$$ as the very structure of fantasy), over the signifier through which it is constituted and from which it is divided (S_1). Each discourse can be produced from the one which precedes it by a quarter turn of its units. Hence Lacan's description of psychoanalysis as the 'hysterisation of discourse . . . the structural introduction via artificial conditions of the discourse of the hysteric' (SXVIII, 3, p. 4). Lacan, therefore, poses analysis against mastery, hysteria against knowing, all of which terms reappear in his account of sexual division in the chapters of *Encore* translated here. Note also the shift away from the earlier formula of language as arbitrary in its effects, to this emphasis on discourse as 'that which determines a form of a social tie' (*E*, pp. 152–3) 'where does the arbitrary come from, if not from a structured discourse' (O, p. 165), a shift which mirrors the change in his account of sexuality towards the specific fantasies which it supports, as described in the introduction (Part II, section II) (tr.).

CHAPTER SEVEN
Seminar of 21 January 1975

Lacan's seminar of 21 January 1975 was published in the third issue of Ornicar?, the periodical of the department of psychoanalysis at the University of Paris VIII. The department was reorganised in 1974–5 under the direction of Lacan and the supervision of Jacques-Alain Miller, who has become increasingly responsible for its administration. It defined its programme as a continuing reassessment of Freud's discovery through the work of Lacan, and the development of closer ties between psychoanalysis and other disciplines (linguistics, logic, topology). Ornicar? was set up to publish information on the department's teaching programme and research projects. It appears five times a year. In Lacan's lifetime, each issue included a draft of Lacan's current seminar.

The seminar that follows, therefore, reflects Lacan's preoccupation with logic and topology, as well as his attempt to construct a possible 'matheme' of psychoanalysis which had come to predominate in his later work. This was defined in the first issue of Ornicar? as the formulation of analytic experience as a structure, against the idea that such experience is ineffable. It appears in this seminar more as an examination of notions such as 'form' and 'consistency', which imply a presence or unity of the subject, and which Lacan opposes with concepts and figures from logic, topology and the formulae of written language, which cannot be cohered in the same way.

In this context, the idea of woman as an object of fantasy is taken further. Lacan argues that woman's position in the sexual relation is that of a 'symptom' for the man, which serves to ward off the unconscious, and to ensure the consistency of his relation to the phallic term. Once again Lacan underlines the precarious nature of any such consistency.

This final article is in many ways elliptical. But it demonstrates the close link between the question of feminine sexuality and that investigation of the foundations of logic and language, which was the constant emphasis of Lacan's work.

The 'Seminar of 21 January 1975' was published in Ornicar? *(Lacan, 1975–   ), 3 (1975), pp. 104–10.*

The question which arises at this point in my exposition is the following, answering to the notion of consistency in so far as consistency presupposes demonstration – what could be supposed to be a demonstration in the real?

Nothing supposes it other than the consistency for which the cord is acting here as the support. The cord is the foundation of accord. And, if I make a leap, I could say that the cord thus becomes the symptom of what the symbolic consists of.

Not a bad formula according to the evidence of language – *wearing down to the thread* [*la corde*], used to designate the wear of the weave. When the thread shows through, it means that the weave is no longer disguised in what is called the fabric. *Fabric* is everywhere and always metaphorical in use – it could easily serve as an image of substance. The formula *wearing down to the thread* clearly alerts us sufficiently to the fact that there is no fabric without weave.

I had prepared for you on paper a whole weave made up uniquely of borromenean knots which could cover the surface of the blackboard. It is easy to see that you end up with a hexagonal pattern. Don't think that by cutting through any one nexus of the weave you would set free any part whatsoever of what it is tied to. If you cut only one ring, then the six rings in between, thereby freed, will be held in place by the six times three (eighteen) other rings to which they are tied in borromenean fashion.

If earlier on I let slip prematurely the term symptom – it being the law of language that something should slip out before it can be commented on – it is precisely because the symbolic provides the simplest metaphor for consistency.

Not that the circular figure is not first of all a figure, that is to say, imaginable, since the notion of good form was founded on this very figure. It is the appropriate notion for making us bring into the real its share of the imaginary. And I would go further – good form and meaning are akin. The order of meaning is naturally configured by what the form of the circle designates as the consistency presupposed to the symbolic. It accords with this, as it were primary, image. It took psychoanalysis to make us see its connection with the order of that body from which the imaginary is suspended.

Who doubts – in point of fact everything called philosophy has to this day hung by this slender thread – that there is an order other than that along which the body thinks it moves. But this order of the body is no more explained for all that. Why does the eye see spherically, when it is indisputably perceived as a sphere, whereas the ear hears sphere just as much, while presenting itself as a spiral?

Would it throw any light on the fact that these two so manifestly differomorphic organs, if I may so put it, perceive spherically if we were to consider things from the angle of my *objet a*? The *petit a* could be said to take a number of forms, with the qualification that in itself it has no form, but can only be thought of predominantly orally or shittily. The common factor of *a* is that of being bound to the orifices of the body. What repercussions, therefore, does the fact that the eye and the ear are orifices have on the fact that perception is spheroidal for both of them?

Without the *petit a*, something is missing from any theory having any possible reference or appearance of harmony. And why? Because the subject is only ever supposed. It is its condition to be only supposable. If it knows anything, it is only by being itself a subject caused by an object – which is not what it knows, that is, what it imagines it knows. The object which causes it is not the other of knowledge [*connaissance*]. The object crosses this other through. The other is thus the Other, which I write with a capital O.

The Other is thus a dual entry matrix. The *petit a* constitutes one of its entries. As for the other, what can be said about it? Is it the One of the signifier?

The idea is at least conceivable, since it did once enable me to couple the One with my *petit a*. On that occasion, I had used the golden number [*or*] to introduce a factor which I had been led to by experience, that is, that between this One and the *a* there is no rationally determinable relation. One can never work out the ratio between the One and the *a*, in other words there is no reason why by placing one over the other it should come out. The remaining difference would be as small as can be figured, it would even have a limit, but within this limit, there would never be any conjunction, any coupling, of One and *a*.

Does that mean that the One of meaning has something to do with the matrix which crosses the Other through with the mark of its double entry? No, for the One of meaning is not to be confused with what makes the One of the signifier.

The One of meaning is the being, the being specified by the unconscious inasmuch as it ex–ists, ex–ists at least to the body, for the striking thing is that it ex-ists in discord. There is nothing in the unconscious which accords with the body. The unconscious is discordant. The unconscious is that which, by speaking, determines the subject as being, but as a being to be crossed through with that metonymy by which I support desire, in so far as it is endlessly impossible to speak as such.

By saying that *a* is that which causes desire, what I mean is that it is not its object. It is not its complement, either direct or indirect, but only that cause which, playing on a word as I did in my first Rome discourse [*Ecrits* (1953)], is always a cause.[1]

The subject is caused by an object, which can be noted only in writing, which is one step forward for theory.

In all this what is irreducible is not an effect of language. The effect of language is the patheme, or passion of the body. But from this language which has no effect, what can be inscribed is that radical abstraction, the object I write with the figure of writing *a*, nothing of which is thinkable – except that everything which is thought of as a subject, the being one imagines as being, is determined by it.

The One of meaning hardly comes into it – it is merely the effect of the One of the signifier, which in fact only works by being available to designate any signified.

As for the imaginary and the real which are here mixed up with the One of the signifier, what can be said about them? What can be said about their quality, what Charles Sanders Peirce calls *firstness*, about what it is that divides them up into different qualities? How, in this instance, can we separate out something like life and death? Who knows where to situate them? – since the One of the signifier comes down as a cause on both sides. It would, therefore, be a mistake to think that it is the imaginary which is mortal and the real which is the living.

Only the common usage of a signifier can be called arbitrary. But where does this arbitrary come from, if not from a structured discourse?

Let me appeal here to the title of a review, which is currently coming out under my auspices at Vincennes – *Ornicar?*[2] It is, surely, an example of determinacy by the signifier. In this case, the fact of being ungrammatical is merely to figure a category of grammar, but, in so doing, the title demonstrates configuration as such, that which, in the eyes of Icarus, merely adorns him. Language is an adorning. It is all rhetoric, as Descartes stresses in the tenth rule. Dialectics can be conceived of only through the usage that it has in relation to a pathematically ordered common use, that is to say, to a discourse associating not the phoneme, even taken in its broadest sense, but the subject determined by being, that is to say, by desire.

What is the affect of ex-isting? (. . . .) What is it, of the unconscious, which makes for ex-istence? It is what I underline with the support of the symptom.

I say the function of the symptom, function to be understood as the f of the mathematical formula $f(x)$. And what is the x? It is that part of the unconscious, which can be translated by a letter, in that only the letter makes it possible to isolate the identity of self to self from any quality.

By underpinning the signifier which the unconscious consists of, each One of the unconscious is capable of being written down by a letter. Doubtless we could do with some convention. But the strange thing is that this is exactly what the symptom, un-controllably, brings about. Hence the aspect of the symptom of never ceasing to be written.

Not long ago, someone I listen to in my practice – and nothing I say to you comes from anywhere else, which is precisely its difficulty – someone articulated something for me, by linking the symptom to the dotted line. The important thing is the reference to writing as a means of situating the repetition of the symptom, as it presents itself in my practice.

The fact that the term came from somewhere else, from the symptom as defined by Marx in the social, does not detract from the appropriateness of its use in, if I may so put it, the private. The fact that the symptom should be defined in the social by unreason doesn't prevent its being distinguished, in the case of the individual, by all kinds of rationalisations. Every rationalisa-tion is a particular rational fact, in the sense not of an exception, but of coming from anyone.

Anyone must be able to be an exception for the function of exception to become a model, but the reverse is not true – the exception does not come to constitute a model by its hanging out with anyone. That is the common state of affairs – anyone can attain the function of exception belonging to the father, which in most cases, as we know, results in its *verwerfung* [foreclosure] through the dependency it gives rise to, with the psychotic result that I have warned against.

A father only has a right to respect, if not love, if the said love, the said respect, is – you won't believe your ears – perversely [*père-versement*][3] orientated, that is to say, come of a woman, an *objet a* who causes his desire.

But what the woman thereby *a*-cquires has no part in the matter. What she busies herself with are other *objet a*, being children, in relation to whom the father does none the less intervene – exceptionally in the best instances – in order to keep under repression, in the happy *me-deum* [*le juste mi-dieu*],[4] his own version of his perversion [*père-version*]. Perversion [*père-version*] being the sole guarantee of his function of father, which is the function of the symptom, as I have written it.

It is enough that he be a model of the function. This is what the father must be, in that he can only be an exception.

The only way for him to be a model of the function is by fulfilling its type. It matters little that he has symptoms provided he adds to them that of paternal perversion [*père-version*], meaning that its cause should be a woman, secured to him in order to bear him children, and that, of these children, whether he wishes to or not, he takes paternal care.

Normality is not paternal virtue par excellence, but merely the happy *me-deum*, mentioned above, that is, the happy un-spoken. Naturally on condition that this un-spoken is not glaringly obvious, that is to say, that one cannot immediately tell what is involved in what it is not saying – which is rare.

Rarely does this happy *me-deum* succeed. Which will enliven the subject when I have time to take it up with you again. But in an article on Schreber [*Ecrits*, (1955–6)], I already made the point to you in passing that there is nothing worse than a father who proffers the law on everything. Above all, spare us any father educators, rather let them be in retreat on any position as master.

I was led to speak to you of *a* woman, since I tell you that *the* woman does not exist.

The woman can perfectly well be delineated, since it is all women, as you might say. But if women are 'not all'? Then if we say that *the* woman is all women, it is an empty set. The advantage of set theory, surely, is that it introduced a measure of seriousness into the use of the term 'all'.

A woman[5] – the question can only be posed from the Other, that is, from that which can be given a definable set, a set which can be defined by what I have written up there on the blackboard as Φ, or the phallus.

The phallus is not phallic *jouissance*. Is it, therefore, *jouissance* without the organ or the organ without *jouissance*? I am putting questions to you in this form in order to give some meaning – regretfully – to this figure. And, making the leap, for whoever is encumbered with the phallus, what is a woman?

A woman is a symptom.

The fact that a woman is a symptom can be seen from the structure which I am in the process of explaining to you, namely, that there is no *jouissance* of the Other as such, no guarantee to be met with in the *jouissance* of the body of the Other, to ensure that enjoying the Other exists. A manifest instance of the hole, or rather of something whose only support is the *objet a* – but always in a mix-up or confusion.

In point of fact a woman is no more an *objet a* than is a man – as I said earlier, she has her own, which she busies herself with, and this has nothing to do with the object by which she sustains herself in any desire whatsoever. To make of this A-Woman a symptom, is to say that phallic *jouissance* is equally her affair, contrary to what is said.

The woman has to undergo no more or less castration than the man. As for what is involved in her function as symptom, she is at exactly the same point as her man. We have yet to articulate what corresponds in her case to that real ex-istence I spoke of earlier as the phallus, the one over which I left you with your tongues hanging out. It has no relation to the little thingummy that Freud talks about.

The dotted lines of the symptom are in fact question marks, so to speak, in the non-relation. This is what justifies my giving you this definition: that what constitutes the symptom – that something which dallies with the unconscious (see Figure 1)[6] – is that one believes in it.

There is so little sexual relation that I recommend you read a very fine novel, *Ondine*.[7] In it you will see that in the life of a man, a woman is something he believes in. He believes there is one, or at times two or three, but the interesting thing is that, unable to believe only in one, he believes in a species, rather like sylphs or water-sprites.

What does it mean to believe in sylphs or water-sprites? Note that one says *believe in*, and that the French language even adds this further emphasis – *croire y*.

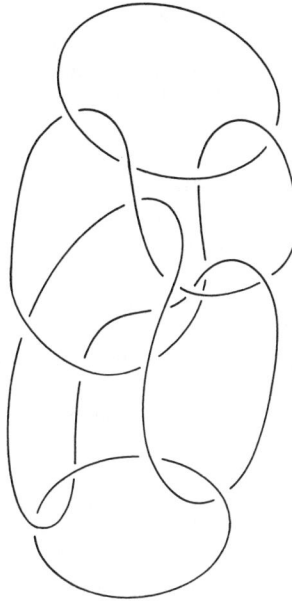

Figure 1

To *believe in*? What does it mean? If not to believe in beings in so far as they are able to say something. I challenge you to find me an exception to that definition. Were one dealing with beings who could not say anything, who could not pronounce what can be distinguished as truth and falsehood, then to believe in them would have no meaning. This goes to show the precariousness of this *believing in*, which the fact of the sexual non-relation manifestly comes down to – a fact not in question, given the overlapping of examples from all sides. Anyone who comes to us with a symptom, believes in it.

If he asks for our assistance or help, it is because he believes that the symptom is capable of saying something, and that it only needs deciphering. The same goes for a woman, except that it can happen that one believes her effectively to be saying something. That's when things get stopped up – to believe *in*, one believes *her*. It's what's called love.

It is in this sense that I have, on occasion, styled the sentiment as comic – that well-known comedy, the comedy of psychosis. Hence the common saying that love is madness.

And yet the difference between believing *in* the symptom and believing *it* is obvious. It is the difference between neurosis and psychosis. In psychosis, not only does the subject believe in the voices, but he believes them. Everything rests on that borderline.

Believing a woman is, thank God, a widespread state – which makes for company, one is no longer all alone, about which love is extremely fussy. Love rarely comes true, as each of us knows, and it only lasts for a time. For what is love other than banging one's head against a wall, since there is no sexual relation?

Love can no doubt be classified according to a certain number of forms, neatly picked out by Stendhal (love as *respect* which is by no means incompatible with *passionate* love, nor with love based on *inclination*), but the chief form of love is based on the fact that we believe her.

We believe her because there has never been any proof that she is not absolutely authentic. But we blind ourselves. This *believing her* serves as a stop-gap to *believing in* – something very seriously open to question. God knows where it leads you to believe there is *One* – it can even lead you so far as to believe that there is *The*,[8] a belief which is fallacious. No one says *the* sylph or *the* water-sprite. There is a water-sprite, a sylph, a spirit, for some people there are spirits, but it all only ever adds up to a plural.

What we need to know now is whether the fact that there is no better way of believing *in*, than to believe *her*, is an absolute necessity.

Today, in relation to the story of the dotted lines, I have introduced the fact that a woman is a symptom. This so matches analytic practice, that, since nobody had said it before, I thought that I had better do so.

Notes

1. *qui cause toujours*: motto of causalist thought, literally 'is always a cause' or 'keeps talking' (tr.).
2. *Ornicar?*: reference to the French expression *Mais où est donc Ornicar?* used to teach school children the use of those conjunctions governing grammatical exceptions (*mais, où, donc, or, ni, car*) (tr.).
3. The French for 'perversely' (*perversement*) has the prefix euphonically equivalent to the noun *père* ('father') (tr.).

4. *mi-dieu*: substituting dieu ('god') in the expression *le juste milieu* ('the happy medium'); later there is a further pun on *dieu* and *dit* (that which is spoken) (tr.).

5. *Une femme*: in French, the indefinite article means both 'a' and 'one'; Lacan is placing *Une femme* ('*A* woman') in opposition to *La femme* ('*The* woman'), and is also marking its relation to the category 'One' which he discusses above (pp. 164–6) (tr.).

6. Lacan's difficulty in many ways became greater in direct proportion to his increasingly elaborated use of the theory of knots which he took from Alexander (1928), and developed in relation to a possible topography of the unconscious in his later work. As regards the texts translated here, the sequence is at one level clear: from the early reference to castration ('we know that the unconscious castration complex has the function of a knot', MP, p. 75) – the insistence on the subjective *and* theoretical difficulty of the concept – to the renewed stress against any myth of imaginary cohesion or consistency ('knots lend themselves with difficulty to the image', SXXI, 9, p. 2). In this second sense Lacan's preoccupation with knots is part of what has been his continuous attempt to find a formula for the difficulty of unconscious processes which is not immediately cancelled by its own immediacy or presence – hence his rejection of geometrical optics in favour of topology ('a set of continuous deformations', SXXI, 6, p. 6), and the recourse to mathematics ('I do not want to write up anything which could be taken for a signified, nor lend to the signified any authority whatsoever', SVIII, 13, p. 5). More recently the theory of knots has been used to stress the relations which bind or link Imaginary, Symbolic and Real, and the subject to each, in a way which avoids any notion of hierarchy, or any priority of any one of the three terms: 'These three terms: what we imagine as a form, what we hold as circular in language, and that which ex-ists in relation both to the imaginary and to language, have led me to bring out the way in which they are linked together' (*Scilicet*, 6/7, 1976, p. 56). Above all, the emphasis is, as always, on the intricate and inextricable nature of the ties which make the subject both subject *of* and *to* the unconscious: 'the unconscious, this knot of our being – the word "knot", rather than the word "being", is the one that matters – the being of this knot which is driven by the unconscious alone' (SXXI, 4, p. 5). We can see this here, in the reference to the symptom (Figure 1) as that 'which dallies with the unconscious' (O, p. 168).

7. *Ondine*, novel by Jean Giraudoux (Paris: Bernard Grasset, 1939) (tr.).

8. *La*: the feminine definite article implying 'The woman' (tr.).

Bibliography

Where original dates of presentation or publication are significant, they are given first in parenthesis.

Psychoanalytic writings

Abraham, K., 'Manifestations of the Female Castration Complex', (1920) *IJPA*, III, 1922, pp. 1–29.

Alexander, F., 'The Castration Complex in the Formation of Character', (1922) *IJPA*, IV, 1923, pp. 11–42.

Andreas-Salomé, Lou, ' "Anal" und "Sexual" ', *Imago*, IV, 1916, pp. 249–73.

Bonaparte, Marie, 'Passivity, Masochism and Femininity', *IJPA*, XVI, 1935, pp. 325–33.

——*Female Sexuality* (London: Imago, 1953).

Brierley, Marjorie, 'Specific Determinants in Feminine Development', *IJPA*, XVII, 1936, pp. 163–80.

Brunswick, Ruth Mack, 'The Pre-Oedipal Phase of the Libido Development', *PQ*, IX, 1940, pp. 293–319.

Chasseguet-Smirgel, Janine, *La Sexualité Feminine, Recherches Psychanalytiques Nouvelles* (Paris: Payot, 1964); trs. *Female Sexuality, New Psychoanalytic Views*, Introduction by Sue Lipschitz (London: Virago, 1981).

Deutsch, Helene, 'The Psychology of Women in Relation to the Functions of Reproduction', *IJPA*, VI, 1925, pp. 405–18.

——'The Significance of Masochism in the Mental Life of Women', *IJPA*, XI, 1930, pp. 48–60.

——'On Female Homosexuality', *PQ*, I, 1932, pp. 484–510.

——'Female Sexuality', *IJPA*, XIX, 1933, pp. 34–56.

——*The Psychology of Women*, vol. I (New York: Grune and Stratton, 1944); vol. II (London: Research Books, 1947).

Fenichel, O, 'The Pregenital Antecedents of the Oedipus Complex', *IJPA*, XII, 1931, pp. 141–66.

——'The Symbolic Equation: Girl = Phallus', *PQ*, XVIII (3), 1949, pp. 303–21.

Freud, Anna, *The Ego and the Mechanisms of Defence* (1936) (London, Hogarth, 1937).

Freud, Sigmund, 'Observation of a Severe Case of Hemi-Anaesthesia in A Hysterical Male' (SE, I, 1886), pp. 21–31.

——'Project for a Scientific Psychology' (1887) (SE, I, 1895), with J. Breuer, *Studies on Hysteria* (SE, II, 1893–5; PF, IV).

——'Fragment of an Analysis of a Case of Hysteria' ('Dora') (1901) (SE, VII, 1905), pp. 1–122 (PF, VIII).

——*Three Essays on the Theory of Sexuality* (SE, VII, 1905), pp. 123–245 (PF, VII).

——'Delusions and Dreams in Jensen's *Gradiva*' (SE, IX, 1906–7), pp. 3–95.

——'On the Sexual Theories of Children' (SE, IX, 1908), pp. 205–26 (PF, VII).

——'Analysis of a Phobia in a Five Year Old Boy' ('Little Hans') (SE, X, 1909), pp. 1–149 (PF, VIII).

——'On the Universal Tendency to Debasement in the Sphere of Love' (Contributions to the Psychology of Love, II) (SE, XI, 1912), pp. 177–90 (PF, VII).

——'The Dynamics of Transference' (Papers on Technique) (SE, XII, 1912), pp. 97–108.

——'On Narcissism: an Introduction' (SE, XIV, 1914), pp. 67–102.

——'Observations on Transference Love' (Papers on Technique) (1914) (SE, XII, 1915), pp. 147–71.

——'Instincts and their Vicissitudes' (Papers on Metapsychology) (SE, XIV, 1915), pp. 109–40.

——'The Unconscious' (Papers on Metapsychology) (SE, XIV, 1915), pp. 161–215.

——'The Taboo of Virginity' (1917) (Contributions to the Psychology of Love, III) (SE, XI, 1918), pp. 193–208 (PF, VII).

——*Beyond the Pleasure Principle* (SE, XVIII, 1920), pp. 3–64.

——'The Infantile Genital Organization: An Interpolation into the Theory of Sexuality' (SE, XIX, 1923), pp. 141–5 (PF, VII).

——'The Dissolution of the Oedipus Complex' (SE, XIX, 1924), pp. 173–9 (PF, VII).

——'Some Psychical Consequences of the Anatomical Distinction Between the Sexes' (SE, XIX, 1925), pp. 243–58 (PF, VII).

——'An Autobiographical Study' (SE, XX, 1925), pp. 3–74.

——*Inhibitions, Symptoms and Anxiety*, (1925) (SE, XX, 1926), pp. 77–175.

——'Female Sexuality' (SE, XXI, 1931), pp. 223–43 (PF, VII).

——'Femininity', Lecture XXXIII, New Introductory Lectures (1932), (SE, XXII, 1933), pp. 112–35.

——'Letter to Carl Müller-Braunschweig' (1935), published as 'Freud and female sexuality: a previously unpublished letter', *Psychiatry*, 1971, pp. 328–9.

——'Analysis Terminable and Interminable' (SE, XXIII, 1937), pp. 209–53.

——'Splitting of the Ego in the Process of Defence' (1938), (SE, XXIII, 1940), pp. 273–8.

Granoff, W. and Perrier, F., *Le Désir et le Féminin*, (1964) (Paris: Aubier Montaigne, 1979).

Horney, Karen, 'On the Genesis of the Castration Complex in Women', *IJPA*, V, 1924, pp. 50–65.

——'Flight from Womanhood', *IJPA*, VII, 1926, pp. 324–39.

——'The Dread of Woman', *IJPA*, XIII, 1932, pp. 348–60.

——'The Denial of the Vagina', *IJPA*, XIV, 1933, pp. 57–70.

——*Feminine Psychology* (London: Routledge and Kegan Paul, 1967).

Irigaray, Luce, *Speculum de l'autre femme* (Paris: Minuit, 1974).

——*Ce Sexe qui n'en est pas un* (Paris: Minuit, 1977).

——'Women's Exile', Interview with Luce Irigaray. *Ideology and Consciousness*, 1, 1977, pp. 24–39.

Jones, E, 'The Theory of Symbolism', *British Journal of Psychology*, IX (2), 1916, pp. 181–229.

——'Notes on Dr Abraham's Article on the Female Castration Complex', *IJPA*, III, 1922, pp. 327–8.

——'The Early Development of Female Sexuality', *IJPA*, VIII, 1927, pp. 459–72.

——'The Phallic Phase', *IJPA*, XIV, 1933, pp. 1–33.

——'Early Female Sexuality', *IJPA*, XVI., 1935, pp. 263–73.

Klein, Melanie, 'Early Stages of the Oedipus Complex', *IJPA*, IX, 1928, pp. 167–80.

——'The Importance of Symbol Formation in the Development of the Ego', *IJPA*, XI, 1930, pp. 23–39.

Lacan, Jacques, 'Le stade du miroir comme formateur de la fonction du Je', (1936) *Ecrits* (Paris: Seuil, 1966), pp. 93–100; *Ecrits: a Selection*, trs. Alan Sheridan (London: Tavistock, 1977), pp. 1–7.

——'Cure psychanalytique à l'aide de la poupée fleur', Comptes rendus, réunion 18 Octobre, *Revue française de la psychanalyse*,

4, October–December, 1949, p. 567.

——'Fonction et champ de la parole et du langage en psychanalyse', (1953) *Ecrits*, pp. 237–322; *Ecrits: a Selection*, pp. 30–113.

——*Les écrits techniques de Freud*: Le séminaire I, 1953–4 (Paris: Seuil, 1975).

——*Le moi dans la théorie de Freud et dans la technique de la psychanalyse*: Le séminaire II, 1954–5 (Paris: Seuil, 1978).

——'D'une question préliminaire à tout traitment possible de la psychose', (1955–6) *Ecrits*, pp. 531–83; *Ecrits: a Selection*, pp. 179–225.

——'L'instance de la lettre dans l'inconscient ou la raison depuis Freud', (1957) *Ecrits*, pp. 493–528; *Ecrits: a Selection*, pp. 146–78.

——'Les formations de l'inconscient' (1957–8), *Bulletin de Psychologie*, II, pp. 1–15.

——'La direction de la cure et les principes de son pouvoir', (1958) *Ecrits*, pp. 585–645; *Ecrits: a Selection*, pp. 226–80.

——'A la mémoire d'Ernest Jones: Sur sa théorie de symbolisme', (1959) *Ecrits*, pp. 697–717.

——'L'éthique de la psychanalyse': Le séminaire VII, 1959–60 (unpublished typescript).

——'Subversion du sujet et dialectique du désir dans l'inconscient freudien', (1960) *Ecrits*, pp. 793–827; *Ecrits: a Selection*, pp. 292–325.

——'Kant avec Sade', (1963) *Ecrits*, pp. 765–90.

——*Les quatres concepts fondamentaux de la psychanalyse*: Le séminaire XI, (1964) (a), (Paris: Seuil, 1973); *The Four Fundamental Concepts of Psycho-Analysis*, trs. Alan Sheridan, ed. Jacques-Alain Miller (London: Hogarth, 1977).

——'Du "Trieb" de Freud et du désir du Psychanalyse', (1964) (b) *Ecrits*, pp. 851–4.

——'L'envers de la psychanalyse': Le séminaire XVIII, 1969–70 (unpublished typescript).

——*Encore*: Le séminaire XX, 1972–3 (Paris: Seuil, 1975).

——'Les non-dupes errent': Le séminaire XXI, 1973–4 (unpublished typescript).

——*Le Scission de 1953: La communauté psychanalytique en France I*, ed. Jacques-Alain Miller, supplement to *Ornicar?* VII, 1976.

——*L'Excommunication: La communauté psychanalytique en*

France II, ed. Jacques-Alain Miller, supplement to *Ornicar?* VIII, 1977.

——*Scilicet*, review of *le champ freudien*, nos. I–VII (Paris: Seuil, 1968–76).

——*Ornicar?* periodical of *le champ freudien*, Dept of Psycho-Analysis at Paris VIII (Vincennes) (Paris, le graphe, no. 1. – , 1975 –).

Lampl-de Groot, Jeanne, 'The Evolution of the Oedipus Complex in Women', *IJPA*, IX, 1928, pp. 332–45.

——'Problems of Femininity', *PQ*, II, 1933, pp. 489–518.

Lemoine-Luccioni, Eugénie, *Partage des Femmes, (le champ freudien)* (Paris: Seuil, 1976).

Mannoni, Maude, *L'enfant, sa 'maladie' et les autres, (le champ freudien)* (Paris: Seuil, 1967); trs. *The Child, his Illness and the Others* (London: Tavistock, 1970).

——*L'ombre et le nom* (Paris: Minuit, 1977).

Montrelay, Michèle, 'Recherches sur la féminité', *Critique*, XXVI, Paris, 1970, pp. 654–74; revised as 'Inquiry into Femininity', trs. with an introduction by Parveen Adams, *m/f*, I, 1978, pp. 65–101.

Müller, Josine, 'A Contribution to the Problem of Libidinal Development of the Genital Phase in Girls', *IJPA*, XIII, 1932, pp. 361–8.

Müller-Braunschweig, C., 'The Genesis of the Feminine Super-Ego', *IJPA*, VII, 1926, pp. 359-62.

Nacht, S., 'Introduction au séminaire de perfectionnement sur la sexualité féminine', *Revue française de psychanalyse*, XXXVII, 1973, pp. 155–63.

Ophuijsen, J.H.W. van, 'Contributions to the Masculinity Complex in Women' (1917), *IJPA*, V, 1924, pp. 39–49.

La Psychanalyse, publication of the Société française de psychana-lyse, (Paris: Presses Universitaires de France, VII, 1964). (Special issue on feminine sexuality).

Rado, S., 'Die Kastrationangst des Weibes', *Internationale Zeitschrift für Psychoanalyse*, XXV, 1935, pp. 598–605.

Rank, O., *The Trauma of Birth* (1924), (London: Kegan Paul, Trench and Trubner, 1929).

Rivière, Joan, 'Womanliness as Mascarade', *IJPA*, X, 1929, pp. 303–13.

Safouan, M., *Etudes sur l'Oedipe, (le champ freudien)* (Paris: Seuil, 1974); 'Is the Oedipus Complex Universal?', trs. Ben

Brewster, *m/f*, 5–6, 1981, pp. 83–90.

——*La sexualité féminine dans la doctrine freudienne, (le champ freudien)* (Paris: Seuil, 1976).

Schneiderman, S. (ed.), *Returning to Freud, Clinical Psychoanalysis in the School of Jacques Lacan* (London: Yale University Press, 1980).

Segal, Hanna, 'Notes on Symbol Formation', *IJPA*, XXXVIII, 1957, pp. 391–7.

Starcke, A., 'The Castration Complex', *IJPA*, II, 1921, pp. 179–201.

Stoller, R., 'A Contribution to the Study of Gender Identity', *IJPA*, XLV, 1965, pp. 220–6.

Winnicott, D.W., 'Mirror-role of Mother and Family in Child Development', (1967) in *Playing and Reality* (London: Tavistock, 1971), pp. 111–18.

Other writings

Alexander, J.W., 'Topological invariants of knots and links', *Transactions of the American Mathematical Society*, XXX, 1928, pp. 275–306.

Benveniste, E., 'La nature des pronoms' (1956), in *Problèmes de linguistique générale*, (Paris: Gallimard, 1966), pp. 251–7; trs. in *Problems in General Linguistics* (Florida: University of Miami Press, 1971), pp. 217–22.

——'De la subjectivité dans le language' (1958), *Problèmes*, pp. 258–66; trs. in *Problems*, pp. 223–30.

Chodorow, Nancy, *The Reproduction of Mothering, Psycho-analysis and the Sociology of Gender* (1978) (London: University of California Press, 1979).

Clément, Catherine, *Vie et légendes de Jacques Lacan* (Paris: Gravet, 1981).

Cowie, Elizabeth, 'Woman as Sign', *m/f*, I, 1978, pp. 49–63.

Fisher, S., *Understanding the Female Orgasm* (Harmondsworth: Penguin Books, 1973).

Hess, T.B. and Linda Nochlin, *Woman as Sex Object, Studies in Erotic Art 1730–1930* (London: Allen Lane, 1973).

Lacoue-Labarthe, P., and J.-L. Nancy, *La titre de la lettre* (Paris: Galilee, 1973).

MacCabe, C. (ed.), *The Talking Cure, Essays in Psychoanalysis and*

Language (London: Macmillan, 1981).

Reiter, Rayna M., (ed.), *Towards an Anthropology of Women* (New York: Monthly Review Press, 1975).

Saint Theresa, *The Complete Works*, ed. Silverio de Santa Teresa P., English edition, Peers (London: Sheed and Ward, 1946).

de Saussure, F., *Cours de linguistique générale* (1915), ed. Tullio de Mauro (Paris: Payot, 1972); *Course in General Linguistics*, (revised ed.) (London: Fontana, 1974).

Sherfey, Mary Jane, *The Nature and Evolution of Female Sexuality* (New York: Random House, 1966).

Turkle, Sherry, *Psychoanalytic Politics: Freud's French Revolution* (New York: Basic Books, 1978).

Index